ROLLING S

CW00642689

Copyright © 1995 Omnibus Press (A Division of Book Sales Limited)

Edited by Chris Charlesworth
Cover & Book designed by 4i Limited
Picture research by Nicola Russell

ISBN: 0.7119.4303.6 Order No: OP47737

Exclusive Distributors
Book Sales Limited, 8/9 Frith Street, London W1V 5TZ, UK.
Music Sales Corporation, 257 Park Avenue South, New York, NY 10010, USA.
Music Sales Pty Limited, 120 Rothschild Avenue, Rosebery NSW 2018, Australia.

To the Music Trade only:
Music Sales Limited, 8/9, Frith Street, London W1V 5TZ, UK.

Photo credits: LFI: front cover; all other pictures supplied by Dezo Hoffman, LFI, Barry Plummer & Pictorial Press.

Every effort has been made to trace the copyright holders of the photographs in this book but one or two were unreachable. We would be grateful if the photographers concerned would contact us.

Printed in Great Britain by Printwise (Haverhill) Limited.

A catalogue record for this book is available from the British Library.

OMNIBUS PRESS
LONDON · NEW YORK · SYDNEY

Contents

Introduction

Beyond the tiny, underground cellar they called the Ealing Club, a dull, post-war culture quietly went on with its business. Inside, a small, stocky figure, studiously hunched over a guitar and styling himself (rather spuriously, given that this was west London, not west Virginia) as Elmo Lewis was blueswailing. It wouldn't have meant much to anyone not wedged inside the overcrowded, sweat'n'smoke-filled joint, but to two teenagers who'd travelled from the other side of town, it was a remarkable sight.

Today, over thirty years later, Mick Jagger and Keith Richards, those awestruck observers who mobbed 'Elmo' and subsequently signed up for his evangelical mission to popularise the music of the black American experience, still play those same sounds. Though since modified by time and technical advances, commercial nous and creative abandon, and a wealth and fame that would have been inconceivable back in 1962, the music of The Rolling Stones has rarely strayed too far from its formative influences. Elmore James, Muddy Waters, Chuck Berry and Jimmy Reed no longer form a significant part of their repertoire, but scratch the surface of their contemporary work and it's obvious that many of the same musical moves – even a little of the bluesmen's perceived 'outlaw' status – remains central to the group's being.

Much else has changed, of course. Elmo Lewis, who quickly reverted to being plain Brian Jones, certainly engineered the Stones' early career. But the blossoming Jagger/Richards song-writing partnership diminished his role, and hastened his departure from the group in 1969. He died shortly after, the dreams of fronting his own R&B outfit unfulfilled to the end. Ironically, the Jones era found the group straying furthest from blues and R&B – and he was the catalyst for

such diversions. Bored with his instrument, the gifted guitarist added textures drawn from Elizabethan madrigals, Eastern scales and the avant-garde to the Stones' music.

His replacement, Mick Taylor, realigned the band to the blues. His virtuoso playing also helped steer them comfortably through an era of changing musical expectations. The rhythm section, adroitly managed by Richards, has always played for feel: Taylor's contribution, often unfairly overlooked, enhanced the band's technical standing at a time when audiences demanded ostentatious dexterity. Unlike their feet-first immersion into psychedelia, the Stones never caught the 'progressive' bug, but Taylor's presence gave their roots-driven approach some credibility.

It's a trick of historical perception that Taylor's replacement, Ronnie Wood, who joined the band in 1976, is still regarded as 'the new boy', even though his period of tenure has far outstripped that of both of his predecessors.

Central to pop's cultural revolution during the Sixties and early Seventies, the Stones have, since the middle of the second decade, become increasingly marginalised. Punk tried to kill them off, while disco, and more recently rap and rave threatened to banish guitar-based rock altogether. But the band – like the bluesmen they once tried to emulate – have been carried along by the weight of their own history. Today, The Rolling Stones are revered as much for their mythological baggage as they are for their music and, incredibly, they're still looked up to by today's hip young guitar-slingers. And that, in a medium which was once dismissed as ephemeral, surely counts for something.

If it's urine-stained garage walls, wrecked hotels and drug-addled bodies you're after, there are already countless publications available that recount the gory details in technicolour. Here, you'll find a comprehensive survey of the music on which those myths hang.

The book is organised into five sections. During the Sixties, the Stones clearly split their work between singles, EPs and albums, and part one reflects that division. Since 1971, the two main formats have co-existed side-by-side, with 45s rarely being issued outside the context of an LP. Consequently, this lengthy period has been divided into two sections; part two, covering the Atlantic era, taking the group up to the watershed of punk rock. Part three picks up the trail in 1978 when, energised by the new wave, by Ronnie Wood's confirmed status and by a lucrative distribution deal with CBS, the band entered a new phase. Part four assesses the live albums, and a short section on compilations concludes the book.

All songs written by Jagger/Richards unless otherwise stated.

DECCA

Part One

The Decca Years 1963-1970

S I N G L E S

The easiest way to access the band's run of singles for Decca during the Sixties is via an American-produced three-CD box set, 'The Rolling Stones Collection: The London Years' (ABKCO 1218-2, 1989). Widely available in the UK, this was assembled by ex-manager Andrew Loog Oldham, who also supervised the digital remastering. It's far from perfect (the remastering was done back in 1989 when the process was still in its infancy), but at the time of writing, it's the most comprehensive survey of the Stones' Sixties singles we've got.

COME ON
(Chuck Berry)
I WANT TO BE LOVED
(Willie Dixon)
(JUNE 1962)

When the band – Mick Jagger (vocals), Keith Richards and Brian Jones (guitars), Bill Wyman (bass) and Charlie Watts (drums) – entered Olympic Sound studios on 10 May 1963, they weren't total novices, having previously taped sessions at Curly Clayton's north London studio and at IBC. But Andrew Loog Oldham, their energetic new manager and self-styled "nasty little upstart tycoon shit" was. When engineer Roger Savage turned to him to discuss mixing the two-track recording, 'producer' Oldham didn't know what he meant, and promptly instructed the engineer to perform the necessary inconvenience himself.

Chuck's original was transformed by a stilted, almost ska-like rhythm, and a hackneyed key-change. Richards even declined to exhibit his carefully-honed Berry licks. What's more, a minor lyrical change ("some stupid jerk" became a "stupid guy") clearly illustrated the will to accommodate the wider listening public.

The flip, a version of Willie Dixon's 'I Want To Be Loved', came straight from their club repertoire, and was a reasonably accomplished performance of a song previously taped at IBC. Aside from Jones' harmonica flourish, and Jagger's delivery of the "Ba-beeh, I wants to be loved" hook (how they must have loved hearing back that line), it still sounded like R&B with a stiff collar and tie on.

I WANNA BE YOUR MAN
(Lennon/McCartney)/
STONED
(Nanker/Phelge)
(NOVEMBER 1963)

The Stones preached R&B on stage and in interviews, but they needed hits to make it count. Good fortune arrived when John and Paul Beatle dropped by at a rehearsal in Ken Colyer's Studio 51 club, and offered them an upbeat rocker destined to become the next 'Ringo track' on their album. In the Stones' hands, 'I Wanna Be Your Man' ripped up the memories of their uncertain début: Bill Wyman's memorable bassline tested the limits of fragile Dansette speakers, while Brian Jones' howling slide unveiled the first signs of an impending musical storm. "Brian made that record with that bottleneck," recalled Keith Richards.

With the 7 October session at De Lane Lea Studios coming to a close, the group had just thirty minutes to deliver a B-side. Surprisingly, perhaps, they eschewed the idea of churning out another well-practised R&B cover in favour of a jam based around Booker T. & the MGs' 'Green Onions'. Pianist Ian Stewart traded blue notes with Keith's guitar, Jones' Delta harp howled menacingly, and Jagger's dilatory "Stoned . . . outta mah mahnd" was delivered in his best Willie Dixon 'Walking The Blues' drawl. Like subsequent group jams, 'Stoned' was credited to the mythical Nanker-Phelge.

NOT FADE AWAY
(Norman Petty/Charles Hardin)/
LITTLE BY LITTLE
(Nanker/Phelge)
(FEBRUARY 1964)

'Not Fade Away' transformed the band into a Top Three act. Buddy Holly's 1957 original already carried the Bo Diddley beat, but the Stones made it count. Hurling their version into a melody-drenched pop arena, they aroused all the latent fears concerning their slavish adherence to what were described as 'jungle rhythms'. It wasn't just the beat, though. It was everything about the record: aggressively played, aggressively mixed, and increasingly aggressively marketed. The Stones' role as the antithesis of The Beatles' homely harmonies was given a dramatic boost.

According to Bill Wyman, Phil Spector didn't shake the maracas, though he did on the B-side, a track from the forthcoming début album (and discussed here in that context). But he doesn't counter the belief that Phil, Gene Pitney and Hollies Allan Clarke and Graham Nash were present at the 10 January 1964 session.

IT'S ALL OVER NOW
(Bobby & Shirley Womack)/
GOOD TIMES, BAD TIMES
(JUNE 1964)

While on their first US tour in mid-1964, the Stones stopped off at Chess recording studios, the centre of the R&B world, where heroes like Muddy Waters, Willie Dixon, Howlin' Wolf and Chuck Berry worked. According to Keith Richards, Muddy was still working there: the band arrived for two days' intensive recording (10/11 June 1964) to apparently find him painting the studio walls.

It was American DJ Murray The K who suggested that the Stones record the Valentinos' recent US R&B hit when they got to Chicago. The excitable country (off)beat was novel, and Jagger and Richards sharing their first chorus together was an important breakthrough, but it was the famously interlocking guitars which remain the song's lasting motif, particularly the spiralling introductory riff, almost muffled out of existence by one too many overdubs. During Keith Richards' hurried break, you can hear an endlessly replayed art college daydream finally catching up with him. He rarely sounded this overwhelmed again. 'It's All Over Now' became the first No. 1 Rolling Stones single.

The flip was an early Dartford station country blues, a trebly recording dating from a Regent Sound Studio session taped on 25 February, towards the end of a UK. tour. It gave the writers their first significant publishing royalty cheque.

LITTLE RED ROOSTER
(Willie Dixon)/
OFF THE HOOK
(NOVEMBER 1964)

One of the band's finest blues covers was taped not in Chicago, but back in central London, at Regent Sound, on 2 September 1964. The performance was wonderfully controlled without ever sounding static, boasted one of their best early productions, and gave Brian Jones the biggest kick in his all-too brief career.

Jones' impassioned bottleneck guitar was the song's distinguishing feature, though the whole arrangement was impressive, smartening up Howlin' Wolf's original almost beyond recognition. It was still a brave decision to release it on single, although the band – prompted by Charlie – won out over Oldham's

initial reluctance. Never again, though. After 'Little Red Rooster', the Stones didn't return to country blues until 1968.

The B-side is discussed in the context of its appearance on the band's second album.

THE LAST TIME/
PLAY WITH FIRE
(Nanker/Phelge)
(FEBRUARY 1965)

Actually, the first time, if it's Jagger/Richards songwriting credits on a Stones' A-side that we're talking about. Securing the No. 1 spot was a major confidence boost, though it was little known at the time that the pleased-as-punch pair had actually borrowed the chorus from The Staple Singers' 'This May Be The Last Time'.

Whereas iffy production threatened to sully 'It's All Over Now', there were no such qualms here. 'The Last Time' was the first single taped at RCA, Hollywood (on 18 January 1965), under the watchful eye of experienced engineer Dave Hassinger, and it positively sparkled. The riff – a characteristic of Jagger/Richards' work – cut right through the song, cruelly emphasising Jagger's relationship-threatening ultimatum.

A new spitefulness, hinted at on the singer's taunting interpretation of 'It's All Over Now', was becoming an integral part of the band's *oeuvre*. 'Play With Fire', originally a rock number titled 'A Mess Of Fire', manifested this dark side in the incongruous setting of tender acoustic ballad, given mock-Tudor trimmings by Jack Nitzsche's joyless harpsichord. This Englishness was accentuated by the lyrics – "She gets her kicks in Stepney/Not in Knightsbridge any more" – encapsulating class-ridden Blighty.

Taped at the end of a lengthy session, 'Play With Fire' (a considerable influence, one imagines, on Arthur Lee's Love) paired Jagger and Richards with Nitzsche and his partner Phil Spector – Watts, Wyman and Jones had fallen asleep.

(I CAN'T GET NO) SATISFACTION/ THE SPIDER AND THE FLY
(AUGUST 1965)

"I'd woken up in the middle of the night, thought of the riff and put it straight down on tape. In the morning... I played it to Mick and said 'the words that go with this are I can't get no satisfaction'." That's Keith Richards on the birth of a quintessential rock anthem, as written in Tampa, Florida, in early May 1965.

He originally envisaged the song as a folk protest number, destined for the 'Out Of Our Heads' album, and that's how it sounded when first recorded at Chess on 10 May.

Two days later, the band returned to RCA and altered the song dramatically. Richards patented the most famous three-note riff in rock on a Gibson fuzz box, Charlie Watts adhered slavishly to a punishing on-beat, and Jagger, in a half-spoken tone that veered from mockery to anger, turned in the performance of a lifetime. His lyrics – "A quasi-Marxist critique of consumerism," according to US critic Robert Palmer, though the first thing Richards did with the royalties was buy a Bentley! – still holds good, too.

Like 'Satisfaction', 'The Spider And The Fly' first appeared in the States – not as a chart-topping 45 but on the US edition of 'Out Of Our Heads'. Warned away from avaricious groupies by their girlfriends at home, the Stones – Charlie excepted – did exactly what you'd expect young Twentysomethings to do. Not everyone would cruelly immortalise such flagrant breaches of trust in song, as the Stones did on this home-grown, mid-tempo blues, taped at the RCA 'Satisfaction' session.

with its declamatory, double-time vocals, and its relentless pursuit to purge every moment of silence from the recording-tape has grown with age.

The B-side is commonly cited as one of the worst Jagger/Richards songs ever to have been blessed with an official release. Certainly, it was closer to being the ugly offspring of their first ballads like 'Tell Me' than it was to the dynamic head of steam the pair had recently been creating. It has a perverse charm, though, not least in the delightfully off-key guitars and flaccid vocals.

GET OFF OF MY CLOUD/ THE SINGER NOT THE SONG

(OCTOBER 1965)

There was a riff in 'Get Off Of My Cloud', but it was buried deep beneath the guitar/bass/drum rhythm – the cloud's 'thunder' if you like. There was also something in the imagery – the world stopping, the guy "dressed up like a Union Jack" wielding a pack of detergent, being 'high' on a cloud – which suggested the presence of strange new influences.

Jagger later said his lyrics were crap, Richards that the song was "one of Andrew's (Oldham) worst productions". But 'Get Off Of My Cloud',

19TH NERVOUS BREAKDOWN/ AS TEARS GO BY

(FEBRUARY 1966)

"Every eight weeks you had to come up with something that said it all in 2:30," complained Keith Richards. That strict discipline didn't always serve the band well on albums or B-sides, where they sometimes skimped on originality, but the same cannot be said of this glorious run of mid-Sixties singles.

'19th Nervous Breakdown', cut in December 1965, a few days after completing yet another gruelling US tour, just about maintained the pace. Hanging on a suitably mis-shapen rockabilly rhythm, the song sparked the usual debates concerning its 'true' meaning. "It's not supposed to mean anything. It's just about a neurotic bird, that's all," Jagger told journalists. Marianne Faithfull is more specific, claiming that Jagger wrote the song after dropping acid with his girlfriend Chrissie Shrimpton. That might explain the "on our first trip" reference, but it doesn't shed any light on why bassman Bill took off on those memorable dive-bombing lines towards the end of the song (or why there's a slight glitch on the fade as the tape momentarily slows down).

Often regarded as the Stones' answer to The Beatles' 'Yesterday', 'As Tears Go By' was actually written a good year earlier, for Marianne Faithfull. It was Jagger and Richards' response to Oldham's request for "a song with brick walls all around it, high windows, and no sex", and had it not been for a keen *Casablanca* fan in the Stones' camp, it would probably still be called 'As Time Goes By'.

The Stones' version was essentially a Jagger/Richards solo collaboration, with Decca's Mike Leander making the most of this rare display of sentiment with a wistful string quartet arrangement. Taped at Regent Sound in London, in October 1965, a new, Italian language vocal was added a few weeks later. That version, released on 45 in Italy, is currently unavailable on CD.

PAINT IT, BLACK/ LONG LONG WHILE
(JUNE 1966)

The presence of a comma after 'It' in the title caused some to speculate that the song was a racist slur. But "neurotic birds" and conventional mores were the band's targets: prompted by their American experiences, their attitude towards racial equality was considerably more advanced than their fellow countryfolk.

The adverts claimed "a different kind of single"; the promotional appearances, with Brian Jones cross-legged and cradling a sitar, did, too. It was: a bleak, bass-heavy lunge into gypsy-styled exoticism, with Bill Wyman on his knees operating the bass pedals on a Hammond organ to great effect.

The flip, also taped in March, returned to the soul-ballad format, albeit with much more confidence in their stride.

HAVE YOU SEEN YOUR MOTHER, BABY, STANDING IN THE SHADOW?/WHO'S DRIVING YOUR PLANE

(SEPTEMBER 1966)

The first Stones' single released on both sides of the Atlantic simultaneously, 'Have You Seen Your Mother' has been described by Jagger as "the ultimate freak-out". He wasn't far wrong, either. 'Mother' encapsulated the indeterminate blur in which the band were forced to live their lives. Its chart life was relatively short, which isn't that surprising, given the uncompromising nature of the song, and its barely coherent production, exaggerated by Mike Leander's manic brass arrangements. Hear the single in stereo on both the 'Singles Collection' box and on 'More Hot Rocks'.

Jack Nitzsche, an ever-present accomplice at the band's RCA sessions, provided the heavy-handed piano on the flip, a Dylan-ish recasting of wigged-out, free-for-all blues.

LET'S SPEND THE NIGHT TOGETHER/RUBY TUESDAY

(JANUARY 1967)

Recorded on 16 November 1966 at a late-night Olympic Studios session for the 'Between The Buttons' album sessions, 'Let's Spend The Night Together' marked a return to safety after the barely-harnessed energy of the previous 45 had confused even the band's most loyal audience.

Written by Jagger after sharing his first night with Marianne Faithfull, the single forfeited the cavernous RCA Studios production style in favour of an up-front piano/bass/percussion sound, with hardly a guitar in sight. Andrew Oldham weaved a yarn about two coppers dropping by and banging their truncheons together on the rhythm track, but more reliable is Keith's memory of Jack Nitzsche fumbling with the piano line on one finger. Most impressive of all was the use of the organ which built steadily throughout the song, so that by the climax, it was the dominant instrument. The Americans weren't impressed with the title, and Jagger was forced to sing 'Let's spend some time together' on the *Ed Sullivan Show*.

Though it ended up with the familiar Jagger/Richards writing credit, 'Ruby Tuesday' began life in Brian Jones' Courtfield Road apartment as a Jones/Richards collaboration. Starting out as 'Title B', a hybrid of Elizabethan lute music and Delta blues, 'Ruby Tuesday' was a sophisticated production, with Wyman and Richards bowing a double bass, and Jones providing the decorative piano and recorder. Jagger's hastily-penned lyric, about a girl who "comes and goes", fitted the mood perfectly.

WE LOVE YOU/DANDELION
(AUGUST 1967)

Bafflingly described as an "artistic nadir" by biographer Philip Norman, 'We Love You' was the odd man out in this run of Sixties singles, but its only failure was only on a commercial level. Ostensibly a "thank you" to the fans who'd supported the Stones through their drug trials earlier that year, it was one of the most extraordinary pieces of music ever committed to 45.

The opening 'walk to the prison cell' introduced a rare slice of *verité* into the pop medium, before wittily cutting to Nicky Hopkins' 'Keystone Cops' piano. From there on, the mood of nervous desperation descended further into chaos. Lennon and McCartney helped out on the backing vocals, Jagger's voice veered between fear and bullishness in roughly equal amounts, but the chief orchestrator was Jones, whose Mellotron and Arabic horn arrangements lent the song an otherworldly glow.

'Dandelion' dated from the 'Between The Buttons' sessions several months earlier, and was a considerably less fraught psych-pop performance (with some distinctly pre-Floydian harmonies). Richards and his girlfriend Anita Pallenberg later named their second child after the song, though she now prefers to be called Angela.

On the original 45, both sides contained brief reprises, which have been kept on the 'Singles Collection' box. But for true stereo versions, you'll have to invest in the 'More Hot Rocks' CD.

JUMPIN' JACK FLASH/ CHILD OF THE MOON
(MAY 1968)

Bill Wyman says he first stumbled across the 'Jumpin' Jack Flash' riff while jamming with Watts and Jones, waiting for the two songwriters to arrive. Weeks later, it reappeared on Keith's guitar, with an accompanying set of lyrics inspired, said Richards, by an elderly gardener with size fourteen feet.

If the lyrics were Dylanish in places, the music has since come to define the quintessential Stones sound: a concise, insistent, sledge-hammer of a riff, harnessed to a simple backbeat and topped with a leery almost mocking vocal. That's why the Stones rarely close a concert without playing it.

A split in the ranks during the 'Satanic Majesties' album sessions grew wider during 1968. The increasingly ostracised Brian Jones was keen to see 'Child Of The Moon' as the band's next 45, but with 'Jumpin' Jack Flash' readily available, there was little chance of that. Nevertheless, the flip – a tough ballad displaying Richards' new open tuning technique – is highly rated by aficionados. Jones, whose contribution was dwindling daily, played sax.

HONKY TONK WOMEN/ YOU CAN'T ALWAYS GET WHAT YOU WANT

(JULY 1969)

Just weeks prior to the release of 'Honky Tonk Women', Brian Jones announced his departure from the band. "The Stones' music is not to my taste any more," ran the official line, though the rootsy rhythm and interlocking country-blues guitars of this song would certainly have met his approval.

Charlie Watts' brilliantly effective bass drum/snare backbeat remains a landmark in rock drumming, all the more so for coming at a time when every musician was judged in terms of ostentatious exhibitionism. New guitarist Mick Taylor made an immediate mark, and the track was laid down in a single day, on 1 June 1969. This, too, has formed an essential part of the Stones' live set ever since.

The flip was a taster from the forthcoming 'Let It Bleed' album, and is discussed in greater detail in that context. It was edited for the single.

THE EPs

The EP format had three main functions: to extend the shelf-life of old single material; to offer selections from from the latest album; or to provide an outlet for themed work not suitable for LP, like live recordings or show tunes. The Stones generally adopted the latter approach, ensuring that there EP material would be exclusive to that format. It's not today, of course, but these songs do end up in odd places.

THE ROLLING STONES
(JANUARY 1964)

With a second single, 'I Wanna Be Your Man', in the bag, the Stones returned to De Lane Lea studios to record their first EP. Unsurprisingly, they decided to cover four recent American hits. The 14 November 1963 session was marred by erratic recording techniques, but with the band's popularity rising rapidly, that didn't hamper the record's success.

All four songs are currently available on 'More Hot Rocks', though one of the versions used is actually an earlier recording.

BYE BYE JOHNNY
(Chuck Berry)

Chuck Berry's sequel to 'Johnny B. Goode' was far less successful, and therefore a prime candidate for the Stones. The engineer appeared to have trouble recording the vocals, but that didn't detract from a first-rate performance, particularly from Richards who ably shadowed Chuck's every lick.

MONEY
(Berry Gordy Jr/Janie Bradford)

A hit for Barrett Strong in 1960, 'Money' had already been covered by The Beatles on their début album, but the Stones found its charms irresistible. So did Bern Elliot and The Fenmen, who took their own version into the UK Top 20 just days after the band had recorded theirs. They shouldn't have bothered – both performance and sound quality were dreadful.

YOU BETTER MOVE ON
(Arthur Alexander)

This concert favourite quickly emerged as the flagship track, suggesting that had it appeared on single, 'You Better Move On' would have been a huge success. But Arthur Alexander's 1962 Southern soul hit wasn't Brian Jones' kind of R&B, and so issuing it on EP provided the perfect compromise. Nevertheless, the Stones give it more than their best shot, with the result that hundreds of up and coming beat groups spent hours practising that sublime major to minor shift in the verse, not to mention the dramatic four note build-up before the middle eight. Definitely among the Stones' best ever covers.

POISON IVY
(Leiber/Stoller)

This was first recorded in August 1963 at Decca's West Hampstead Studios with young staff producer Michael Barclay, and had been slated for the band's second single. However, things didn't quite go to plan, as Dick Rowe recalled: "It was a disaster. The Stones thought Mike was a fuddy-duddy. He thought they were mad."

There was nothing mad about the finished recording, where the Stones resembled a Merseybeat combo, right down to the vacuous harmonies. 'Poison Ivy' was hastily dropped from the schedules. They tried it again in November, and were sufficiently pleased with the results to include it here. This slower version is now conspicuous by its absence, for it's the colourless original, first aired on the 'Saturday Club' compilation, which is readily available on 'More Hot Rocks'.

FIVE BY FIVE
(AUGUST 1964)

'Five By Five' was the best memento the band could have brought back from their inaugural American visit. This five-track EP was the first fruits of their two-day session at Chess in Chicago, and with Ron Malo at the controls and many other legendary hands to shake, the group finally fulfilled a dream. Awestruck? It didn't show.

IF YOU NEED ME
(Wilson Pickett/Robert Bateman/Sonny Sanders)

They dispensed with the horns favoured by Wilson Pickett and Solomon Burke, both of whom covered the song in 1963, but there was no mistaking the song's deep gospel origins, helped along by Ian Stewart's organ-playing.

EMPTY HEART
(Nanker/Phelge)

Before exhibiting their profligate attitude towards women, Jagger/Richards relied on memories of adolescent yearning to fire their imaginations. 'Empty Heart', recorded on the second day of their intensive sessions at Chess Studios in Chicago, was passable R&B, with some impressive harmonica playing.

2120 SOUTH MICHIGAN AVENUE
(Nanker/Phelge)

Basically a jam hinging on a funky R&B bassline, '2120 South Michigan Avenue' was a musical tribute to Chess Studios – the title was simply the blues Mecca's full address. Once again, Jones took the lead with some blueswailing harmonica, with some strong competition from Ian Stewart on organ.

CONFESSIN' THE BLUES
(Walter Brown/Jay McShann)

Originally an early Forties swing jazz number by pianist Jay McShann and vocalist Walter Brown, 'Confessin' The Blues' was overhauled by Chuck Berry in 1960, from which the Stones took their cue. Having played it regularly since their July 1962 live début, the band were confident with their arrangement, and it showed.

AROUND AND AROUND
(Chuck Berry)

Back in April 1962, a bedroom band named Little Boy Blue and The Blue Boys – featuring Jagger, Richards and future Pretty Thing Dick Taylor – posted a tape to Alexis Korner. It included a version of Chuck Berry's 'Around And Around'. Little over two years later, the two first-named were recording at Chess in the presence of Chuck himself.

Eager to impress the assembled Godheads, the Stones turned in a tight, near-flawless performance, as Richards revealed himself as a master of Berry's technique. Stu's piano fills lent greater authenticity to the demonstration of R&B, London-style.

GOT LIVE IF YOU WANT IT!
(JUNE 1965)

Glyn Johns recorded the first three shows of the Stones' March 1965 UK tour, at the Regal, Edmonton (5 March), the Empire, Liverpool (6), and at the Palace, Manchester (7). To achieve the right amount of *verité*, he slung a microphone into the audience. The results weren't too good, but with so little live material in existence from the early years, 'Got Live If You Want It!' (a play on Slim Harpo's 'Got Love If You Want It') remains a priceless document.

WE WANT THE STONES
(Nanker/Phelge)

Not content with their share of the ticket money, the band craftily claimed publishing royalties on an audience's impromptu chant. So far, this piece of social history has eluded CD release.

EVERYBODY NEEDS SOMEBODY TO LOVE
(Bert Russell/Solomon Burke/Jerry Wexler)

The opening track from the new 'No. 2' album was an obvious choice for the tour, but it was severely edited for this release.

PAIN IN MY HEART
(Otis Redding/Phil Walden)

'Pain In My Heart' was one of two ballads performed on the Spring 1965 tour. The other was 'Time Is On My Side'.

(GET YOUR KICKS ON) ROUTE 66
(Bobby Troup)

When Keith Richards began his solo, the audience erupted, but probably not in appreciation of his virtuosity: my money's on Jagger's leg-twitching James Brown impression. This live version appears on 'December's Children'.

I'M MOVING ON
(Clarence E. Snow)

This was particularly welcome, because there's no evidence that the Stones ever recorded it in a studio. They twisted country star Hank Snow's 1950 original into a really vicious stage number, though if truth be told, they probably learnt it from Ray Charles, or via the skiffle circuit. But nothing could have touched this, which climaxed in an ungodly orgy of noise. Today, you'll find this proto-metal recording on 'December's Children'.

I'M ALRIGHT
(Nanker/Phelge)

This track had become part of the set six months earlier, and was basically an excuse for Jagger and Jones to compete for the fans' attentions. It can be found on the 'Out Of Our Heads' CD.

THE ALBUMS

The CDs covering the Decca period follow the American London Records' catalogue. Yet, back in the Sixties, the Stones themselves were baffled by the incoherent approach used to sell their music to the most lucrative market in the world. Yet it worked, and today that market has got so used to its own crazy chronology that it's now become the official line. Pick up a handful of early Stones CDs, and you'll get a totally misleading picture of their early development. Currently in the racks are at least six titles which should not be there.

a) '12 x 5' (London 820 048-2), which utilises the same cover photo as the original UK 'No. 2' album, shares just four songs with the second album proper, the rest being made up of EP and single material, and one song, 'Congratulations', which was exclusive to the set.

b) 'The Rolling Stones, Now!' (London 820 133-2)', was the third US album, but shared around 50% of its material with the UK 'No. 2' album. It also included 'I Need You Baby (Mona)', omitted from the US version of the début LP, jumped the gun with 'Heart Of Stone', which didn't appear in the UK until several months later, and added 'Little Red Rooster' and another 'exclusive' non-UK title, the dismal 'Surprise, Surprise'. Recorded at Regent Sound in May 1964 this first appeared on the various artist 'Fourteen' compilation.

c) 'Out Of Our Heads' (London 820 049-2) is particularly irritating because though it shares the same title with the UK original, it's no less a bastardisation than any of its predecessors. Again, some 50% of the material is shared, but this boasted four sides from two recent singles, a track from the live EP, and another non-UK Jagger/Richards off-cut, 'One More Try', taped at RCA in May 1965.

d) 'December's Children (And Everybody's)' (London 820 135-2) is probably the most incoherent of the lot. Sporting the 'Out Of Our Heads' cover shot, it blends four tracks from the UK edition of that album with an ill-fitting musical patchwork. This included isolated songs from EPs and singles, plus two songs deemed unsuitable for the UK market – a Chess recording of Muddy Waters' 'Look What You've Done', and 'Blue Turns To Grey', a string-laden Jagger/Richards original, taped in January 1965 and later covered by Cliff Richard.

e) 'Between The Buttons' (London 820 138-2) was close, but no cigar I'm afraid for including the 'Let's Spend The Night Together'/'Ruby Tuesday' 45 at the expense of 'Back Street Girl' and 'Please Go Home'.

f) 'Flowers' (London 820 139-2) had no identity at all: it's merely an opportunist collection of mid-Sixties material from various sources. It's interesting for the inclusion of three songs which didn't see the light of day in the UK at the time: a version of Smokey Robinson's 'My Girl', which was a waste of recording tape; and two late '66 Jagger/Richards songs intended for other artists, 'Ride On Baby' and 'Sittin' On A Fence'.

Now that the post-1971 catalogue has been treated with care by new licensees Virgin, and bearing in mind that the 'digital remastered' state of these London discs (not to mention the packaging) is woefully out-of-date, the Stones' Sixties material requires a complete overhaul. (I'm not even convinced that the best possible masters have been located for these CDs.) If and when such a reappraisal happens, the track listings should conform to the albums as originally issued in the UK. Here they are...

DECCA

The Rolling Stones

(UK CD: LONDON 820 047-2, RELEASED APRIL 1964)

All four Beatles held corporate smiles for the cover of their first album: the Stones remained unsmiling, aloof, even anonymous - Andrew Oldham was adamant that the group name stayed off. Buoyed by the incremental success of their first three singles, the lone, self titled EP, and the screams which greeted the band's first nationwide tour, he was only a few minutes early when his sleeve-notes proclaimed - with typical arrogance - that his charges were "more than just a group... a way of life".

The dramatic cultural shifts which altered the expectations of teenagers and problematised their relationship with authority didn't happen because of The Rolling Stones. But the group who simply began life wanting to give the world a music lesson unwittingly got caught in the eye of a socio-political tornado; and over the next few years, one generation's hopes, and another's fears, were largely assumed to lay within the Stones' collective body.

Musically, this self-titled début album lay closer to the heart of the group's original, evangelical intentions than it did the future sound of marching, charging youth in revolt. The implicit threat posed by the cover was nourished by some of the material – the sound of barely-controlled urges on 'I Just Want To Make Love To You', the uncivilised beat of 'Mona' and the metaphor-rich 'I'm A King Bee', for example.

Yet, right from the start, the Stones understood that musical palettes would only be enlightened gradually. This meant supplementing their beatified covers of unsung R&B with material already tried-and-tested on the American pop charts, like Marvin Gaye's 'Can I Get A Witness', which had a proven track record but remained relatively obscure at home. Most revealingly, the band's own attempts to write material were a far cry from roughly-hewn R&B or even mild social critique, as 'Tell Me' amply illustrates.

Recorded on a two-track Revox at Regent Sound, during January and early February 1964, 'The Rolling Stones' was essentially a one-take re-creation of their stage act. Taped with the minimum of fuss it nevertheless created the maximum impact, knocking The Beatles off the top of the album charts and reputedly selling 100,000 copies in its first week of release.

In America, it was retitled 'England's Newest Hitmakers – The Rolling Stones', with 'Not Fade Away' replacing 'Mona (I Need You Baby)'. But, despite the troublesome transfer to CD of the Stones' mid-Sixties albums, the current London disc carries the same material as the UK original.

ROUTE 66
(Bobby Troup)

Originally a US hit for Nat 'King' Cole in 1946, under its full title, '(Get Your Kicks On) Route 66', the Stones learnt this from Chuck Berry. They stuck faithfully to his version, toughening it up as any enthusiastic five-piece fresh from doing battle with screaming audiences would

do. For several months, they'd heard Jagger count off those near-mythical destinations – St. Louis, Missouri, and "oh so pretty" Oklahoma City. But as they struggled to keep the beat tight, without surrendering the song's raw energy, those names – and the transatlantic fantasies they suggested – began to assume a more concrete aspect. Soon, it was the band's lives which began to resemble the product of a fertile imagination.

I JUST WANT TO MAKE LOVE TO YOU
(Willie Dixon)

If Chess Records was a car, with label boss Leonard Chess behind the wheel and Muddy Waters his star passenger, then the back-seat driver must have been Willie Dixon. A veteran of countless recording sessions, as musician and producer, Dixon also wrote. His misfortune was that other artists invariably made his songs their own, and while he titled his autobiography 'I Am The Blues' with some justification, he never received the acclaim afforded to many of his contemporaries.

The Stones were no different, and probably learnt 'I Just Want To Make Love To You' from Muddy Waters. Sounding like five virgins desperate to end their enforced celibacy, the band put the recording equipment to the test, with Jagger's vocals and Jones' harp in particular regularly forcing the levels into the red. The engineer, perhaps getting into the spirit of the thing, left the scrappy ending on the fade-out.

HONEST I DO
(Jimmy Reed)

The fledgling Stones performed five Jimmy Reed numbers at their Marquee début, and while these had been gradually dropped in favour of more up-tempo material, it would have been unthinkable not to have included any of Reed's work on their first album.

Having already recorded his 'Close Together' and 'Bright Lights, Big City' prior to the Decca deal, they opted for this 1957 recording when it came to officially sanctioning Reed's work. Centring around some nimble, if at times precarious Richards/Jones interplay, the song also revealed Jagger's Dartford-on-Mississippi blues drawl at close hand.

I NEED YOU BABY
(Mona) (Ellas McDaniel)

Probably the album's centrepiece, this imaginative interpretation of the Diddley beat clearly showed how rhythm and texture lay at the heart of the Stones' *oeuvre*, in contrast to The Beatles who, with George Martin's encouragement, were primarily concerned with melodic and harmonic arrangements.

Even Bo himself was moved to comment on Brian Jones' impressively-controlled reverb effect on the guitar track, which neatly interlocked with an assortment of percussion – drums, maracas, tambourine, handclaps – enthusiastically bashing out the infamous Diddley shuffle. A week later, the band employed the same rhythm, with far greater commercial results, on 'Not Fade Away'.

NOW I'VE GOT A WITNESS
(Like Uncle Phil and Uncle Gene) (Phelge)

Having achieved their best take of Marvin Gaye's 'Can I Get A Witness', the band decided to have some instrumental fun with the riff. Stu switched from piano to a wheezy organ, Jones, Richards and Wyman muscled in with instrumental breaks, and a tambourine-waving Jagger beat time alongside Watts.

Later that day (4 February), as the group began to celebrate the end of the album sessions, and with several famous pals in attendance, the air turned blue for the unreleased 'Fucking Andrew' (alias 'Andrew's Blues').

LITTLE BY LITTLE
(Phelge/Phil Spector)

First heard on the flip of 'Not Fade Away', 'Little By Little' also dated from the lively 4 February session. So lively, in fact, that there is some confusion as to whether it was Gene Pitney (as the sleeve stated) or Stu on piano, though most sources agree that Phil Spector, who received a writer's credit alongside the band's mysterious Mr. Phelge, shook the maracas. Keith Richards' solo was spirited if a bit ropey (probably the cognac that had begun to flow freely), but even that couldn't distract from the fact that the song was basically a rewrite of Jimmy Reed's 'Shame, Shame, Shame'.

I'M A KING BEE
(James Moore)

In 1968, Jagger effectively disowned the band's copycat days when he said, "What's the point in listening to us doing 'I'm A King Bee', when you can hear Slim Harpo doing it?" Perhaps it was no coincidence that this track also featured one of the most upfront vocals on the entire album, revealing a detectable nasal twang to Jagger's voice. Bill Wyman admirably recreated Fats Perrodin's sliding bass, while Jones's slide stung just as effectively as Harpo's 1957 version.

CAROL
(Chuck Berry)

'Carol', like 'Mona' and 'Route 66', was one of the first tracks recorded for the album, just days after the group rehearsed it for inclusion in their live set. It's archetypal Berry: classic four-bar guitar intro, verses divided by vocal calls and guitar responses, lyrics that merged performing, dancing and romancing into one thoroughly modern art, and a killer of a chorus.

When Keith Richards presented Chuck with the first award at the Rock'n'Roll Hall Of Fame in 1986, he confessed: "I lifted every lick he ever played." He cashed in several of them on this thrilling performance.

TELL ME
(YOU'RE COMING BACK)

"Our first songs were terrible," admitted Jagger, with the benefit of hindsight. Not all of them: after all, Gene Pitney had turned one of the very first, 'That Girl Belongs To Yesterday', into Top 10 material before 1963 was out.

The missionary zeal which found the Stones consuming American blues and R&B at an alarming rate largely eradicated any thoughts of developing their own songwriting. But realising that music publishing was the most lucrative wing of the industry, Andrew Oldham locked the two likeliest candidates in a room together and told them not to emerge until they'd written a song.

'Tell Me' wasn't the first (the ineffective 'It Should Be You', covered by George Bean, pipped it by a couple of months), but it bore out Jagger's early claim that home-grown R&B would be pointless. Instead, the songwriting Stones opted for pure pop balladry – gentle and sentimental, except that their own handling of the material was, as 'Tell Me' clearly shows, hamfisted and unconvincing. Strangely, it took off abroad when issued on single, and they were still playing it on tour as late as March 1965.

Aside from being the first official (Jagger/Richards) Stones' song, 'Tell Me' is most notable for Keith's cavernous, Hank Marvin-like twang during the break. The version issued on this CD is longer than the take used on the original UK album, retaining a scrappy, unfaded ending. (For the original fade, check out the 'More Hot Rocks' CD.)

CAN I GET A WITNESS
(Eddie Holland/Lamont Dozier/Brian Holland)

The Beatles endorsed the new Detroit sound by including three Motown covers on their second album, 'With The Beatles', issued in November 1963. The Stones were unwilling to be left behind, and so Jagger was sent to Denmark Street to locate the sheet music for one of the label's more recent US hits, by newcomer Marvin Gaye.

However, the Stones were no match for The Beatles in the harmony stakes, and Jagger's thin, unconfident voice no substitute for Gaye's rich tones. It wasn't the last

time they'd come unstuck covering contemporary American material.

YOU CAN MAKE IT IF YOU TRY
(Ted Jarrett)

Jagger warmed up for his later Otis Redding impressions with a near-histrionic performance on this version of Gene Allison's 1957 calm soul ballad. While purists complained that much got lost in the translation, it's also true that the homegrown R&B groups added something the originals could never hope to capture. On such misunderstandings was the British beat boom born.

WALKING THE DOG
(Rufus Thomas)

Just in case anyone received the wrong message via the surly faces on the album sleeve, the band played out with a cover of Rufus Thomas's novelty hit, complete with shrill whistles and daft backing vocals. So the Stones were a fun-chasin' bunch after all, though that Richards boy sounded dead serious about his solo.

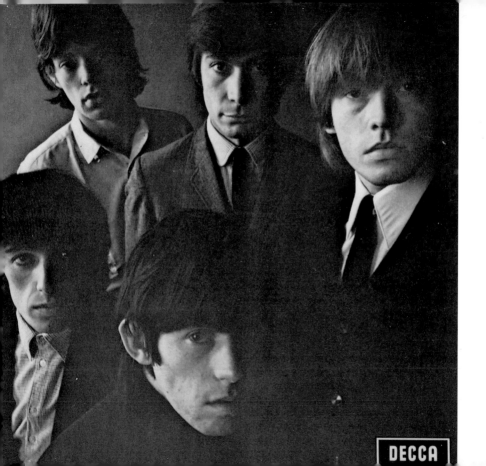

DECCA

The Rolling Stones No.2

(JANUARY 1965)

American material once again formed the basis of a Stones album, though with one key difference. Most of the songs they chose were recent hits. With dozens of home-grown R&B acts sifting through the Chess archive for potential songs, and Jagger and Richards still in the formative stages of their songwriting, the Stones inevitably turned to the Billboard R&B charts for inspiration. There they found contemporary songs by Otis Redding, Solomon Burke, The Drifters and Irma Thomas – none of which had made any impact in the UK – crying out to be covered.

The début album was completed during a couple of intensive bouts of recording at Regent Sound Studios. 'No. 2' reflected the band's new-found worldliness, drawing from sessions taped in London (Regent), Chicago (Chess) and Hollywood (RCA). While the first LP had been a set of contrasts – fast-paced rock'n'roll and unhurried blues or ballads – 'No. 2' was more a measured affair, lacking the exhilarating moments of raw energy of its predecessor. The major ructions came courtesy of Andrew Oldham's state-of-the-Stones-nation address on the rear sleeve. One line, "See that blind man, knock him on the head," didn't exactly impress parents or politicians, already animated by the moral panics surrounding Ton-Up Boys and Mods. The matter of Oldham's street-wise hip-speak was even raised in the Lords. Meanwhile, the album flew out of the racks.

EVERYBODY NEEDS SOMEBODY TO LOVE
(Bert Russell/Solomon Burke/Jerry Wexler)

No sooner had Solomon Burke committed his version to vinyl than the Stones decided to cover it. The song provided an upbeat start to the album, and was slightly unusual in that it clocked in at just under five minutes. The version which is most readily accessible on CD now (on

'The Rolling Stones, Now!') is the demo originally issued by mistake in the States. It's considerably shorter, more hurried and sports backing vocals of a very questionable nature. The track dates from the band's first session at the spacious RCA Studios in Hollywood, where Elvis recorded many of his hits.

DOWN HOME GIRL
(Jerry Leiber/Jerry Butler)

Few outside a coterie of enthusiasts were familiar with Alvin Robinson's original, and the Stones' hackwork probably didn't inspire too many of their own fans to investigate further.

YOU CAN'T CATCH ME
(Chuck Berry)

Endorsement by The Beatles and the Stones clearly had an effect. After Chuck Berry's 'Let It Rock' and 'Memphis Tennessee' coupling charted late in 1963, 'No Particular Place To Go' went a few places better, securing a Top Three placing the next Spring. 'You Can't Catch Me', culled from one of Chuck's neglected singles, and originally issued in

November 1956, was little known over here, and therefore ripe for covering. Pity they didn't think of it when selecting their début single.

TIME IS ON MY SIDE
(Norman Meade/James Norman)

The band stuck fairly closely to Irma Thomas's original, issued in the States earlier in the year, although this version – taped at Chess in November 1964 dispenses with Ian Stewart's gospel organ, which dominated the band's first stab at the song, taped at Regent Sound back in May. The 'Vol. 2' performance also featured a more prominent guitar line, a mark of the band's improving powers of interpretation.

Since its return to the band's live set in 1981, the song has taken on a distinctly new meaning, as a haughty display of durability. For the original UK cut, check out the 'Singles Collection' or 'Hot Rocks 1964-1971'. The US 'gospel' version appears on '12 x 5'.

WHAT A SHAME
(Jagger/Richards)

You hear more detail on the stereo version found on 'The Rolling Stones, Now!' CD, but there are some painful flaws – chiefly distortion – in the original master which spoil the effect. Written in the down-home Chicago blues style, the band even tried to pass off their own brand of 'trouble in mind': "you might wake up in the mornin'/Find your poor self dead".

GROWN UP WRONG
(Jagger/Richards)

Bluesmen like John Lee Hooker and Howlin' Wolf defied conventional time-signatures with artful abandon. The Stones couldn't hope to mimic Wolf's 'Forty Four' or Hooker's 'Boogie Chillen', so they stuck to a regular beat and tried to graft an off-beat rhythm over the top of it. That didn't quite work, as 'Grown Up Wrong' clearly shows, but it gave Brian Jones another opportunity to display his bottleneck technique.

DOWN THE ROAD APIECE
(Don Raye)

Something of a standard during the Forties, this number probably swung best when in the hands of pianist Merrill Moore, who covered it in 1955. The Stones based their version on Chuck Berry's 1960 recording, and had been playing it ever since their live début in 1962. They rarely did Berry a disservice when covering his songs, or even his interpretations of others' material, and 'Down The Road Apiece' is mighty impressive. The rhythm section, with Ian Stewart in tow, swung effectively, but it's Keith Richards – who gets more fired-up with each guitar break – who shines most. "Wow, you guys are really getting it on," Berry is supposed to have said as he watched the band recording it at Chess in June 1964.

UNDER THE BOARDWALK
(Artie Resnick/Kenny Young)

Apparently taped on the same day as 'Little Red Rooster', this version of a recent Drifters' US hit recreated the song's hot summer ambience, but sent those who'd heard the original into paroxysms of anxiety nevertheless.

Competing with one of the most gifted vocal groups in the business was one surefire way to gain an inferiority complex. A more generous assessment is that the Stones were still evangelising. That said, this version topped the Australian charts early in 1965.

I CAN'T BE SATISFIED
(Muddy Waters)

Such was the shambles of the band's London catalogue that American audiences didn't get to hear this – the first official tribute to the man whose 'Rolling Stone' had once given Brian Jones an idea – at the time. And it was Jones' slide guitar which gave the Stones' second album its most authentic blues moment. Not that authenticity really entered into it: in the minds of their audience, the Stones didn't have to be judged in terms of their peers.

For a true stereo version, check out the 'More Hot Rocks' CD.

PAIN IN MY HEART
(Otis Redding/Phil Walden)

This slow, aching ballad had been a minor hit for the big-voiced, but little-known Southern soul singer Otis Redding in 1963. Despite the writing credits, the song was originally penned by Naomi Neville (alias Allen Toussaint) and first recorded by Irma Thomas as 'Ruler Of My Heart'.

In contrast to the days when the band could virtually play their favoured R&B standards in their sleep, many of the soul covers on their second and third albums resulted from raids on specialist record stores while in the States: heard one day, recorded the next, and probably forgotten the day after. 'Pain In My Heart', marked by a mean Bill Wyman bassline, and taped at RCA in early November 1965, ended up in the band's set for a while.

OFF THE HOOK

'Off The Hook' was the band's first truly impressive version of a Jagger/Richards-penned song, even though the bassline came straight from Motown and the guitar riff was R&B cut with Chuck Berry's rock'n'roll vision. The lyrics (written with some assistance from

'Scottish' Dave Thompson) betrayed the first signs of 'women problems' that would develop into an unrestrained misogyny over the ensuing months. The recording dates from the 'Little Red Rooster' session.

SUZIE-Q
(Eleonore Broadwater/Stanley Lewis/ Dale Hawkins)

The album closed in fine style, with this sweaty reworking of Dale Hawkins' 1957 US hit. Watts was first out of the starting-block with a memorable drum pattern, the cue for some cutting guitar exchanges (roll over Chuck Berry), and those preposterous handclaps. Sadly, it was all too short, and 'Suzie-Q' was over almost before it began.

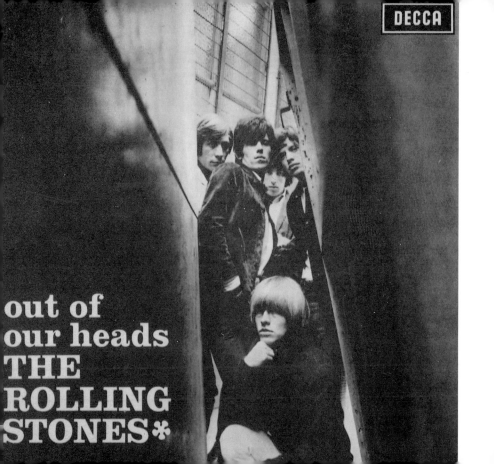

Out Of Our Heads

(SEPTEMBER 1965)

Unlike 'No. 2', which was pieced together from songs recorded in three corners of the world, 'Out Of Our Heads' was very much the first album taped at the RCA studios in Hollywood. "We loved this studio because it was custom-built with no windows," recalled Bill Wyman. "We neither knew nor cared whether it was night or day but just kept playing on."

Compared with the makeshift studios they'd been used to, RCA was a microcosm of America itself – a seemingly endless expanse, stuffed with all manner of expensive gadgets and worldly staff. The band returned to the studio many times during the next two years, recording several of their best-known hits there. But on 'Out Of Our Heads', the relationship had yet to flourish. Sure, the band taped 'The Last Time', 'Satisfaction' and 'Get Off Of My Cloud' during the making of the album, and each was a singularly unique creation. But a combination of lukewarm material and some hasty production work rendered 'Heads' a marking-time album. It showed little

development, apart from an almost total exclusion ban on country blues (no equivalent of 'I Can't Be Satisfied', for example), and that wasn't necessarily a good thing.

SHE SAID YEAH
(Jackson/Christy)

Speciality artist Larry Williams is best known for 'Short Fat Fannie', for providing The Beatles with 'Bad Boy', and for taking his own life in 1980. 'She Said Yeah' wasn't one of his major hits, even after the Stones had condensed it into ninety seconds of shocking, ultra-metallic rhythm and blues.

MERCY, MERCY
(Don Covay/Ronnie Miller)

An R&B hit for Don Covay earlier in the year, 'Mercy, Mercy' was first tackled by the band at a leisurely Sunday session at Chess in November 1964. This one definitely had that RCA ring about it, and that's probably because it was re-recorded there on 10 May 1965.

HITCH HIKE
(Marvin Gaye/William Stevenson/Clarence Paul)

This was cut at the very first RCA session, and the band were buoyant with the results, despite the rushed circumstances of the recording. 'Hitch Hike' was the Stones' second Marvin Gaye cover, and was an improvement on their earlier reading of 'Can I Get A Witness'. The main disappointment was that the Stones were happy to turn in passable covers of American material until they'd written some good material of their own.

THAT'S HOW STRONG MY LOVE IS
(Roosevelt Jamison)

The band loved the sound they got at RCA, but by the time 'Out Of Our Heads' had been mixed, it was the work taped at Chess which was most impressive. One of those to benefit was 'That's How Strong My Love Is', which boasted a tremendous performance from Jagger.

GOOD TIMES
(Sam Cooke)

Covering light material like this 1964 Sam Cooke hit was a far cry from ripping up audiences with twenty-minute versions of 'Hey, Crawdaddy', and indicated just how desperate the group were to cling to their success. 'Good Times' was recorded at RCA on 13 May 1965.

GOTTA GET AWAY
(Jagger/Richards)

Too many recording sessions squeezed between too many concerts didn't always yield the best results, as this moderate Jagger/Richards song confirmed. The riff was later used for the live arrangement of 'Under My Thumb', as chillingly heard at the Altamont Festival, and captured on *Gimme Shelter*.

TALKIN' 'BOUT YOU
(Chuck Berry)

This cover had been in the set since early 1964, though it wasn't recorded commercially until September 1965. It was not one of their better Berry covers, partly because it was taken at half-speed, partly because it wasn't suited to the RCA ambience.

CRY TO ME
(Bert Russell)

Solomon Burke first covered this country-soul ballad in 1962, but for those who'd not heard his version, Jagger's belting performance was impressive enough. 'Cry To Me' was one of six cuts taped at RCA on 13 May 1965: 'Satisfaction' was another.

OH BABY
(WE GOT A GOOD
THING GOIN')
(Barbara Lynn Ozen)

America heard this several months before the home audience, when it appeared on 'The Rolling Stones, Now!' in February 1965. Once again, it was the usual R&B hit hackwork, dashed off as soon as they'd learnt it from the 45, and then quickly forgotten about.

HEART OF STONE

Unlike the wall of sound which had begun to characterise the singles, the early experiments with stereo clearly exposed the roughness of the individual parts. The heavily-reverbed tambourine beat sagged, the backing vocals were weak and Jagger's theatrical vocal was inclined to hit distortion levels. But at least the stereo version (on 'The Rolling Stones, Now!') isn't as muffled as the mono recording on the 'Singles Collection' box.

Not even those shortcomings could direct attention away from this popular – and most persuasive Jagger/Richards – ballad. An earlier version, which appears on 'Metamorphosis', was recorded in July at Kingsway Studios, London, but the definitive take was bagged at RCA early in November.

THE UNDER ASSISTANT WEST COAST PROMOTION MAN
(Nanker/Phelge)

Another upfront Chess recording lost in a sea of barely-penetrable RCA cuts, this song had previously appeared on the flip of

'Satisfaction', albeit in a slightly different form. The riff was identical to the cover of 'Fannie Mae', taped on the same day, which suggests that 'Under Assistant' was direct steal. The lyrics, which were the band's own, had some fun at the expense of George Sherlock, the real-life London Records promo man who accompanied the Stones on their first US tour.

I'M FREE
(Jagger/Richards)

This must have been written before the endless tours, the interminable recording sessions, the inane interviews, the anonymous hotel rooms, even the demanding girls, all became a chore. That was when they discovered that freedom wasn't quite as simple as they'd made it sound on this splendidly carefree arrangement, taped at the August '65 'Get Off Of My Cloud' session. The song made a surprise reappearance at the July 1969 Hyde Park concert.

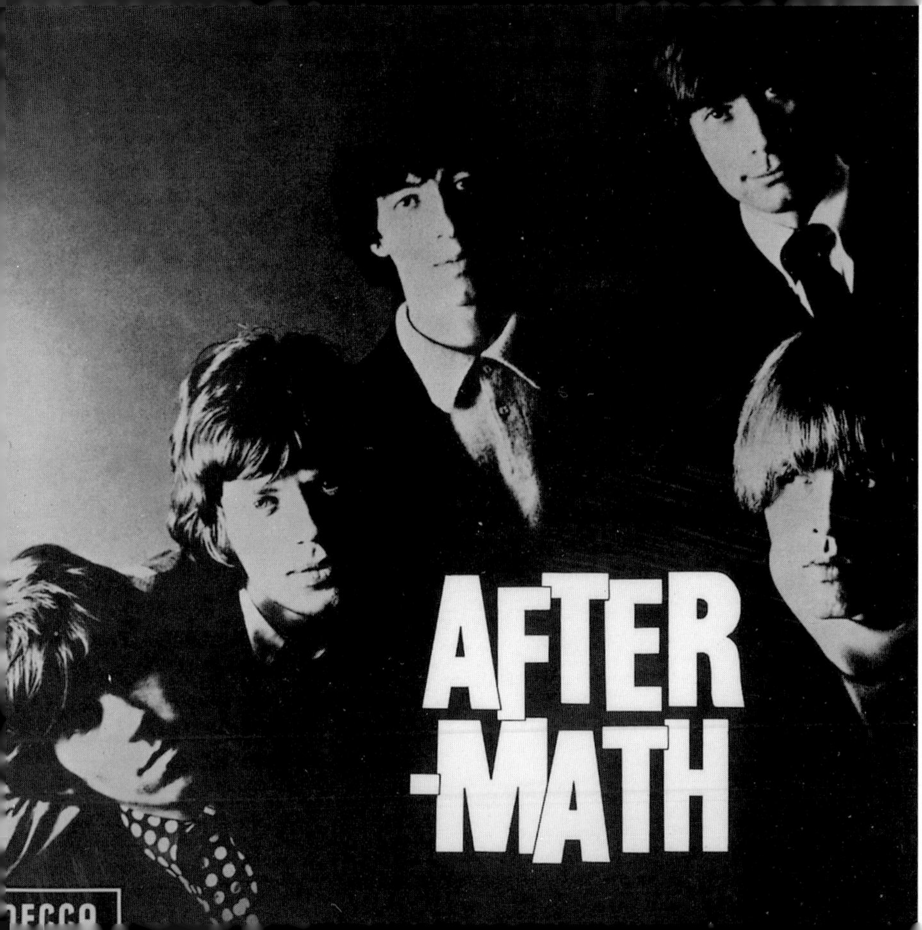
AFTER
-MATH

Aftermath

(LONDON 820 050-2, RELEASED APRIL 1966)

'Aftermath' was the first Stones album that didn't sound like a hastily assembled tribute to the sounds of black America. Whereas just four self-penned songs were deemed strong enough for inclusion on 'Out Of Our Heads' – one of those a jam – 'Aftermath' dished up fourteen new Jagger/Richards titles, with not a cover version in sight.

The R&B/beat boom was maturing fast. Inspired by The Beatles' example, everyone wanted to become an author. Bands who didn't write their own material were second-class citizens, and if you weren't at Bob Dylan's Royal Albert Hall performance, well...

The evolution of 'Satisfaction' proved that it took only a slight shift of emphasis (or a lucky break like stumbling across a fuzz-pedal) to transform potential album filler material into a hit single. This precarious situation prevailed during the making of 'Aftermath', a record which quite clearly contained its fair share of stinkers wedged between the evergreens.

As if to enhance the band's standing as 'creators' rather than the increasingly maligned 'interpreters', Andrew Oldham forfeited the opportunity to make obscure cultural references about the Stones' importance and offend the nation's power brokers in his customary sleeve-note. Instead, that honour fell to RCA in-house engineer Dave Hassinger, who wrote: "In this business of dubious standards, it's been great working with the Stones, who, contrary to the countless jibes of mediocre comedians all over the world (*Dean Martin, Come On Down!*), are real professionals and a gas to work with."

Certainly, the arrangements were far more imaginative than before, the production was clearer, and at least half the songs confirmed the Jagger/Richards songwriting team as worthy of comparison with Lennon/McCartney, and talented new arrivals like Pete Townshend and Ray Davies. But the most interesting aspect of the album was its Englishness – harpsichords and dulcimers lent an Elizabethan air to several of the songs, while one track, the ground-breaking 'Goin' Home' gave a clear indication of the band's homesickness.

Recorded during two lengthy sessions, in December 1965 and March 1966, several of the songs had been destined for an earlier release, provocatively titled 'Could YOU Walk On The Water?'. That was nixed by a combination of Decca's outrage and a new batch of material taped by the band.

MOTHER'S LITTLE HELPER

What better way to make a pitch for the young generation's hearts than by kicking off their new record with a derisory groan guaranteed to enrage the elders and excite those whose time was about to come? "What a drag it is getting old" was every bit the equal to "I can't get no satisfaction", and Jagger's surly delivery made a real meals-on-wheels of it.

Yet 'Mother's Little Helper' was not merely another excuse to prise open the 'generation gap', but a condemnation of crass middle-class, middle-age values which compelled hypochondriac housewives to dose up on pills because "the pursuit of happiness just seems a bore". The sickness that the protagonist in 'Satisfaction' observed is also here, the "instant cakes" and "frozen steaks" which, far from producing a leisure culture, creates a generation of dependants in dire need of medication in order to alleviate their inability to cope with freedom. It's a typically miserable – and misogynist (the husband is present only in terms of his needs) – Jagger lyric, but the suburban nightmare is lent a touch of exoticism by a simple sitar motif, played by Brian Jones.

Subsequently issued as a US 45, 'Mother's Little Helper' was first aired on 'Today's Pop Symphony' by 'The Aranbee Pop Symphony Orchestra Under The Direction Of Keith Richard', a front for yet another of Andrew Oldham's projects.

STUPID GIRL

First the mother, next the daughter. Compared with the dramatic opener, this is throwaway, and nonsense throwaway at that. It's been said that the Stones' perception of women took a turn for the worse after encountering lofty débutantes whose disregard

for uncultured pop groups punctured the band's egos. But dressing up ignorant sexism in terms of a wider class struggle just won't do: the only suggestion that irony may lie at the heart of the song is the absurd Blackpool-pier-type organ, rendering 'Stupid Girl' as archaic as its lyric content. The line about "a lady in waiting to a virgin queen" was further evidence of an unfolding Elizabethan subtext.

LADY JANE

That subtext – a discovery of a quaintly English, as opposed to a distant American culture – was made explicit in this surprisingly tender ballad, given mock-Tudor trimmings by Brian Jones' dulcimer and Jack Nitzsche's harpsichord.

Reporters were told that the song had been based on a letter written by King Henry VIII to Jane Seymour; Jagger's girlfriend Chrissie Shrimpton thought it was a veiled love song to her; while his biographer Anthony Scaduto claimed it was based on rich girl-about-town Jane Ormsby-Gore. Andrew Oldham had written a song called 'Sir Edward And Lady Jane' for the Mighty Avengers several months earlier, so it might well be traced back to him.

UNDER MY THUMB

Shrimpton was less inclined to claim that she inspired this vicious put-down, but Marianne Faithfull seems to think that's precisely who it was aimed at.

Subtle guitar work and Jones' light marimba touches undercut the vitriolic lyrics (sample line: "Under my thumb's a squirming dog who's just had her day").

The song later gained notoriety when The Who recorded it (and 'The Last Time') to keep the Stones' music before the public after the 1967 drug busts. Two years later, festival-goer Meredith Hunter was stabbed to death at Altamont during the song.

DONCHA BOTHER ME

Turning round fourteen songs for an album while in the midst of an American tour must have stretched the patience, as this one-riff take on country blues indicated.

GOIN' HOME

Long considered a pivotal moment in pop's slow transmutation into rock, 'Goin' Home' was a jam that took the blues as its starting-point and ended up crashing the three-minute barrier purely because no-one signalled when to stop. Frankly, it doesn't achieve much during its eleven-minute duration, especially when compared to the improvisations undertaken in the name of psychedelia months later. But it broke the mould in two senses – temporally, and in the Yankophiles' yearning to return to London.

Ostensibly a one-off, the song was performed in concert during the March 1967 European tour, before being usurped by the considerably more dextrous 'Midnight Rambler'.

FLIGHT 505

Buddy Holly's influence wasn't purely musical. The memory of a pop star in his prime downed in a plane crash lingered long in the collective memory: the glamour of being photographed in the VIP lounge prior to departure was no doubt followed by uncharacteristic twinges of vulnerability while boarding the jet. 'Flight 505' is propelled by a light, almost jocular rhythm,

and while Jagger makes light of the seaward-end for the passenger who seconds earlier is "feeling like a king", the song reflected an acute awareness of travel being one of the hazards of the job.

HIGH AND DRY

Country music, yes, but which country? Jagger had learned how to emulate the harsh, Southern drawl (those 'r's!), but Keith's primitive guitar picking was closer to the folk-rock popularised by The Seekers and probably more indigenous to Britain. The message, though, was familiar: my girl gone done me no good.

OUT OF TIME

And she gone done it again! Chris Farlowe had the hit with it, a soulful rendition which was as much a lament as anything else. Jagger's version was nowhere near as compassionate, his wagging, accusing finger prodding home the message that unfaithfulness means goodbye.

IT'S NOT EASY

Fuzz bass was used several times on the album, but it gave the record – and this good-time boogie in particular – a really dated feel. The song, which tackles the rather un-Stoneslike subject of loneliness, pales badly when held up against Brian Wilson's 'In My Room', or Lennon's 'Help!', but it was probably never intended as anything other than filler.

I AM WAITING

Not so this inspired mood piece which, by a 'bouncing voices' effect, mirrored by Jones' gentle dulcimer playing and Wyman's eerie bassline, remains one of the band's most extraordinary mid-Sixties compositions, blowing hot and cold with remarkable subtlety.

TAKE IT OR LEAVE IT

'Aftermath' is noted for being the first completely self-composed Rolling Stones album, but it was inconsistent. Following the ambitious 'I Am Waiting' with this 1964-styled pop song, destined to be covered by The Searchers, seems an extraordinary *faux pas* in retrospect.

The track first appeared on the aforementioned 'Today's Pop Symphony' LP.

THINK

Years later, the Stones had learnt the lesson that albums should always finish on a high-note. 'Aftermath' was obviously organised on a different basis, for 'Think', wedged between two similarly substandard tunes, ensured that the record cooled down with a whimper. Once again, the song was destined for another singer, but even Chris Farlowe struggled to do much with it.

WHAT TO DO

What better inspiration for Mick to write a paean to boredom than this insignificant tune, which again indicated that the reservoir of good Jagger/Richards songs was hardly inexhaustible.

DECCA

Between The Buttons

(JANUARY 1957)

For the first time since their début, the Stones recorded an album almost exclusively in London. But while sessions for that first album had been hastily stolen in between a hectic touring schedule, the atmosphere of 'Between The Buttons' was quite different. "Dopey camaraderie," is how Bill Wyman describes the mood at London's Olympic studios during November and December 1966.

The industrious sessions at RCA and Chess, when the main concern was to bag as many songs as possible, with little knowledge of where they might end up, had been left behind for good. Instead, 'Buttons' was built up over several weeks in party-like conditions, with many pals – Robert Fraser, Anita Pallenberg and Marianne Faithfull, Tony Sanchez, Michael Cooper, Gered Mankowitz, Jimi Hendrix, Tara Browne, Nicky Hopkins, even Peter Cook and Dudley Moore, showing up.

Despite two of the best tracks – 'Back Street Girl' and 'Please Go Home' – being left off in favour of both sides of the 'Let's Spend The Night Together' single, 'Between The Buttons' has always been popular with American critics, who no doubt preferred its exotic Englishness to the tough blend of R&B and contemporary soul covers, which they'd heard all before anyway.

'Buttons' found the Stones drifting further away from the safety-net of black American music. The sound was as claustrophobic as ever, but now benefited from advances in studio techniques, Bob Dylan, dope and a more relaxed approach to songwriting. The leap into an indistinct future was mirrored by Gered Mankowitz's Vaseline-enhanced cover photo, which depicted a discernible fuzziness around the edges. It wasn't too long before that vagueness began to gnaw at the band's core.

YESTERDAY'S PAPERS

Compared to George Martin's Beatles productions, the Stones' work always teetered on the edge of messdom. This opening track continued where they'd left off with the 'Have You Seen...' single. Call-and-response vocals, an occasional glockenspiel, fuzzed guitars and a busy bassline might have cluttered the song (a "horrible public humiliation" of Jagger's ex, Chrissie Shrimpton, according to Marianne Faithfull), but it maintained the sense of whirlwind confusion that had infected their glorious run of mid-Sixties singles. Despite this, it was the only 'Buttons' track to be played live when the group toured Europe in March.

MY OBSESSION

The claustrophobia of living in and out of each other's pockets while on a seemingly never-ending régime of concert tours and studio sessions found its way into this song. Unusually, it's a simple drum riff and a particularly high-in-the-mix bassline – which provides the musical backbone, though Ian Stewart fills in with some slightly incongruous boogie-woogie phrases. Apparently written several

months before the 'Buttons' sessions began in the autumn, 'My Obsession' gave another insight into the damaged mental health of a band forced to live life at an extraordinary pace.

BACK STREET GIRL

A waltz rhythm, gently picked acoustic guitar, delicate glockenspiel and a Parisienne accordion helped make 'Back Street Girl' one of the band's most successful ventures into musical loveliness. But what were those words? "Don't want you part of my world/Just you be my back street girl" added the typical touch of cruelty, just in case any enlightened soul imagined they'd heard the sound of a new leaf turning.

CONNECTION

The better stereo separation afforded by CD reveals the incredibly naïve production on what once sounded full-bodied through a Dansette speaker. Performed live, as it was on the controversial *Sunday Night At The Palladium* TV appearance on 22 January 1967, the song would have cohered better. Here, it sounds oddly pedestrian, despite being one of the more sprightly numbers on the album.

Like much of their future work, 'Connection' is an out-and-out drug song: "they're dying to add me to their collection" seems in hindsight rather prophetic, bearing in mind that within weeks of the recording, three of the group would become scapegoats for an entire, drug-wise generation.

SHE SMILED SWEETLY

Virtually free of the invective that made almost every Stones 'girl' song a poison pen letter, 'She Smiled Sweetly' – featuring Keith Richards on organ – was the most direct recognition of Bob Dylan's hold over the aristocracy of British beat. Like much of the record, it abounds with contradictions, not least the tenderness in Jagger's voice being undercut by the aggressive bassline. The overall effect, dominated by the heavy organ and strong chord changes, is akin to the members of the Hellfire Club holding a themed 'gospel' night.

COOL, CALM AND COLLECTED

Taking their cue from The Kinks' fascination for music-hall, with Jagger adopting an upper-class twit persona, the Stones took this peculiarly short-lived sub-genre a stage or two further, throwing in a stop-start chorus, sitar embellishments and even a race-to-the-end finale. Perhaps it was no coincidence that the newly-recruited pianist was Nicky Hopkins, fresh from working on The Kinks' 'Face To Face' album sessions.

There's a possibility that parts of this song were initially taped at RCA in August, although even if this was the case, the track was – like the rest of the album – finished at Olympic during November and December 1966.

ALL SOLD OUT

Another number which doesn't necessarily benefit from the close scrutiny of the CD format. While the band's RCA productions, cavernous and dense as they often were, usually ended up as greater than the individual parts, the 'Buttons' sessions – with the band and Oldham fumbling together in the control room – were notoriously unsuccessful in mixing the individual four-track recordings coherently. Not that this meant that the album lacked individuality: on the contrary, its wilful amateurism makes it sound all the more extraordinary in the light of today's highly ordered recording techniques.

One of the few tracks to carry a strident guitar track, 'All Sold Out' found Jagger reverting to his familiar role as hard-done-by-boy on the offensive. The backing vocals, fleeting recorder notes and anti-climactic middle-eight all capture that spur-of-the-moment feeling, which is exactly what this album filler – entertaining though it may be – obviously is.

WHO'S BEEN SLEEPING HERE?

Dylan's influence on the Stones never shone as brightly as on this quaintly English fable of infidelity. Brian Jones reputedly once jammed with pop's premier poet so hard that his harmonica-puffing lips bled. All turned out for Mr. Zimmerman's infamous concert at the Royal Albert Hall. And all forward-thinking R&B bands were keen to show an acquaintance with folk-rock, and for Dylan's knack of introducing a string of unlikely characters into song, adding new vistas of interpretation that would previously not have been there.

PLEASE GO HOME

This psychedelicised reworking of the Diddley beat should have been a single, though the slight downturn in sales of the band's 45s during 1966 probably put paid to that. Oscillating wildly in a way that made 'Not Fade Away' seem positively leaden, 'Please Go Home' was fronted by a vibrant, highly-distorted guitar, drew on a range of studio effects, and gave Charlie the perfect excuse to bash hell out of his cymbals. One of the band's most undervalued performances.

COMPLICATED

"She knows just how to please her man/She's softer than a baby lamb/But she's very educated/And doesn't give a damn". Faithfull, too, by any chance? 'Complicated', with its freakbeat fuzz-guitar, chiming organ and psych-pop harmonies, was the rich man's Dave Dee, Dozy, Beaky, Mick and Tich.

MISS AMANDA JONES

Good use was made of stereo separation, and of the increasing capacity to overdub additional instrumentation on 'Buttons'. 'Miss Amanda Jones' was a sterling example of both – beneath the song's insistent melody, there's a miasma of sound vying for attention.

SOMETHING HAPPENED TO ME YESTERDAY

Given the events just around the corner, this vaudevillian celebration of the disorientating effects of acid, juxtaposed with satirical jabs at the British bobby, proved rather damning. There was a moral there: don't take Sergeant Dixon's (Of Dock Green) name in vain.

The British groups' special relationship with America was fast-becoming supplanted by a re-acquaintance with the fading artefacts of their own culture. It was a similar quest for the archaic which resulted in The Beatles' 'Sgt. Pepper' a few months later.

DECCA

Their Satanic Majesties Request

(LONDON 820 129-2, DECEMBER 1967)

Since the day it appeared, this album has been regarded as the joker in the Stones' pack. A misguided answer to The Beatles' 'Sgt. Pepper'? The inevitable result of too much acid and too few musical ideas? Or simply a case of the Stones just not looking right in kaftans. The critical onslaught was relentless: "The most dreadful collection of songs the band had ever released," wrote Jagger biographer Anthony Scaduto. Nik Cohn was similarly unimpressed, calling it "toothless... and boring." Even Keith Richards dismissed it as "a load of crap".

They're all wrong, of course. 'Satanic Majesties', wayward and unfocused as it was, captured the commercial lunacy inherent in acid's topsy-turvy inversion of the real world in a way 'Sgt. Pepper', 'When I'm 64' and all that, never could. With no George Martin to cast a disapproving eye over the bodies strewn across the studio floor, or to bring a semblance of musical order to the proceedings, the Stones ditched producer Andrew Oldham and, with Glyn Johns' role restricted to simply getting the sounds down on tape, revelled in their new-found freedom.

One only has to look at the expression on Brian Jones' face, on the promo film shot in the studio to accompany 'We Love You', to realise that this was no rich band's ersatz psychedelia cash-in. The deep sense of paranoia and persecution generated by the band's well-publicised drug busts created a siege mentality within the Olympic studio walls. Unsurprisingly, then, sessions were protracted and unpredictable – on several occasions, Charlie Watts and Bill Wyman turned up only to discover that the unholy trinity of Jagger, Richards and Jones were otherwise indisposed.

This goes some way to explaining the ragged glory of the finished product, where drugs, mysticism, musical uncertainties, personal catastrophes and the incipient beginnings of a hotline to Satanism conspired to create probably the most well-rounded evocation of an acid-inspired world. Five R&B enthusiasts in their mid-Twenties, making tentative explorations into inner and outer space, with seemingly every musical instrument under the sun at their disposal, would have been unimaginable only months earlier. But with the long arm of British (in)justice bearing down on them, the Stones were growing up fast, forced into becoming 'spokesmen of their generation', and yet inside, wondering just how Andrew Oldham's publicity had backfired in their faces. 'Satanic Majesties' (the title itself doubling as a 'fuck you' to their persecutors, and a bluesman/outsider's response to the eras of joint-induced conviviality) was undoubtedly the malformed product of a very difficult birth: shocking to behold, but strangely worth a hundred cheerfully bouncing sonic babies. The idiot bastard offspring of psychedelia, it was – unsurprisingly – the punk rockers' favourite 'hippie' album a decade or so later.

SING THIS ALL TOGETHER

Part of the appeal of the Delta blues, particularly for white boys living in London, was its apparent communion with forces hitherto undiscovered by the rational world. That hallucinogenics unblocked similar force-fields clearly provided the inspiration for this initiation into the Stones' grave new world. The power of collective music-making and a sprinkling of psychedelic wisdom could, 'Sing This All Together' suggests, enable us "to see where we all come from". Humankind's essential being, no less, is the quest, as the song invokes a mythical state of nature where drums are beaten, where caves are covered in paintings, and where the pictures that emerge "show that we're all one".

'Sing This All Together' starts as the album means to go on: loose arrangements, introspective pseudo-Taoism and untamed spirits. There's no Beatles-like guarantee that you'll "enjoy the show", only that an electronically-induced sense of time-warp disorientation just might play havoc with your sense of "the now". Bearing in mind the band's recent traumas, it's little wonder that 'Satanic Majesties' is littered with the language of escape.

Vignettes drawn from Jagger's brushes with snooty débutantes are nowhere to be heard.

CITADEL

Segued with the previous track (it's a 'Pepper'-like concept album!), 'Citadel' opens with a characteristic Richards riff which provides one of the few links with the Stones' previous work. But the way Charlie Watts assaults his kit, hitting his cymbals like never before or since, and the reflective pause between each verse disrupt any sense of familiarity. If it's the old R&B outsiderism, then it's in a different guise: more stranger in a strange land, than any 'whole world's down on me' homily.

'Citadel' milks the well-worn '1984' scenario, with anti-capitalist messages ("flags are flying dollar bills") set alongside anti-authoritarianism (the peasants hearing "their numbers called") and futuristic nightmare scenarios (cars flying "through the woods of steel and glass"). The Mellotron sound that undercuts the chorus could well solve the mystery behind the 'Fairground' title apparently cut at the sessions; being remarkably similar to the music that accompanies merry-go-round rides.

IN ANOTHER LAND
(Bill Wyman)

Flags didn't only fly dollar bills in 1967: they also heralded a first. Bill Wyman broke the Jagger/Richards songwriting stranglehold with this impressive song, written on one of those lonely nights when the big boys failed to materialise.

Bill already had several production credits to his name, but he – like Brian Jones – was aggrieved at the unwillingness of the Jagger/Richards/Oldham triumvirate to entertain the idea of another songwriting Stone. No matter: this unlikely fusion of mediaeval harpsichord music, Orientalism and Syd Barrett-like innocence has long been a favourite among fans, not least in the States, where – because it was the closest thing to a ballad on the album – it appeared on single.

Written and demoed by Wyman at home early in July, and originally titled 'Acid In The Grass', the basis was taped by Bill, Charlie Watts and Nicky Hopkins on 13 July. Not being a singer, Wyman suggested that a tremolo effect be used on his vocal track, which was further buttressed when The Small Faces' Steve Marriott was hauled in from an adjoining studio to sing backing vocals. Next day, Mick and Keith liked what they heard, with the proviso that they add their voices on the chorus. This enhanced the song's schizophrenia mirrored by the dream-like verses and 'awake' chorus. The snoring at the end is Wyman's, taped in the control room in September.

2000 MAN

More futuristic, 'The Prisoner'-type projections of a society made up by numbers, not people, but nothing alters in the customary abuse of women: husbands now conduct their illicit affairs with computers. '2000 Man' was one of the more tightly constructed songs on the album, a direct advance on the tentative, more structured experimentation of 'Between The Buttons'. The chorus sits uneasily with the rest of the song, but what the hell: with repeated listens, as the recorded medium allows, even the apparently random can appear natural after a few plays.

SING THIS ALL TOGETHER
(See What Happens)

'Goin' Home' might have been longer, but this eight-minute plus epic was the nearest the Stones ever got to free-form improvisation. After some self-conscious conversation at the start of the track ("Where's that joint?" says Jagger. "Flower Power, eh?" jests another), the only vocal sounds heard are sighs, chants and a crescendo of screams. Towards the end, there's an attempt to touch base as a verse from 'Sing This Altogether' is reprised (flashback-style, again a technique used on 'Pepper'), but glockenspiel and flute notes hover gently, brass instruments rumble audaciously, and the assorted percussion pounds haphazardly in this exercise in song deconstruction.

Nearer to the maverick Texans Red Krayola than to the more musically-conscious San Francisco bands, the track exits with the seasonal 'We Wish You A Merry Christmas' message, doctored beyond all recognition by Bill Wyman. (At one stage, the album was going to be titled 'Cosmic Christmas'.) Oddly, in this year of love and peace, it faded with the slowed and highly treated voices chorusing the words, "We hate you". Well, it certainly sounded like it. As Charlie once said, the band never looked right in kaftans anyway.

SHE'S A RAINBOW

Perched precariously with the instincts of a ballad but the bite of a rock number, 'She's A Rainbow', which started out as 'Lady Fair', has a place of its own in the Stones' catalogue. After the opening montage of street-market sounds ('real life' often found its way into psychedelic work), Nicky Hopkins' Mozart-like piano figure set the tone – delicate and beguiling, evoking the song's subject, the girl who's curved and colourful, just like a rainbow, in fact.

Violins and cellos (arranged by future Led Zeppelin bassist John Paul Jones) augment the strident rock beat, while some trickery on the 'Munchkin'-like backing vocals intensify the overall air of unreality.

THE LANTERN

Although the tendency was to overdub as many instruments as the Olympic studio four-track could possibly handle, 'The Lantern' was slow and dirge-like, a sum of sparse individual parts which, on close inspection, revealed a lax approach to mixing. 'Majesties' was, after all, Jagger and Richards' first real attempt at production. This song, which gives the light/darkness metaphor further mileage, lays bare the fragments (even Keith flicking his pick-up switch). Technical buffs might hang their heads in horror, but the effect conveys well the perspective-altering hallucinogenic world-view.

GOMPER

Samuel Gompers was a leading 19th century American labour leader, a fact that probably has nothing to do with the title whatsoever: the song's true inspiration comes from the East. After going through the motions of a song, with Jones' sitar trading riffs with Richards' guitar, this turns out to be merely the launching-pad for a lengthy, raga-inspired jam, with Eastern flutes, spacey organ and Moroccan hand drums creating the most exotic moments on what's certainly the band's most exotic record.

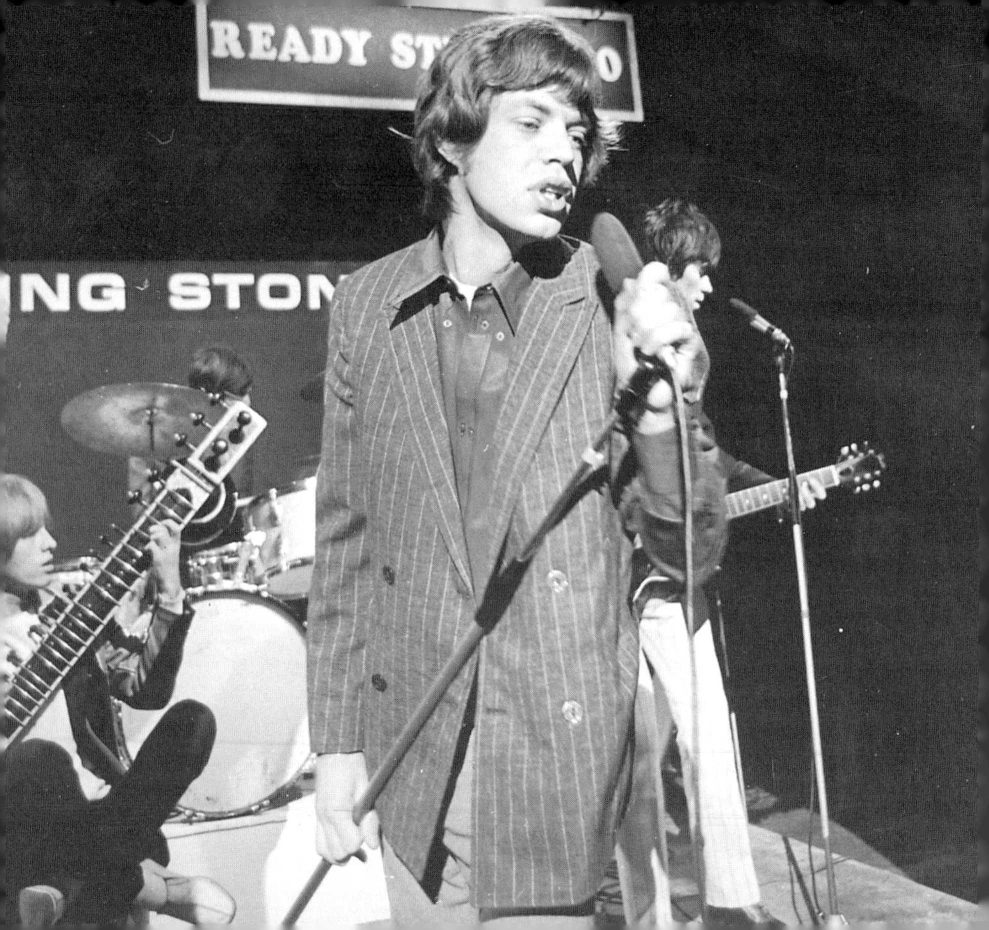
READY

2000 LIGHT YEARS FROM HOME

Mick Jagger apparently wrote these lyrics while in his Brixton Prison cell. Even the preferential champagne and caviar couldn't hide his despondency but instead of penning a powerful piece of social critique, he opted for the soft option: a cosmic 'We've Gotta Get Out Of This Place'.

The result was the most enduring track on the record: its tight, measured arrangement contrasted well with Jones' ghostly Mellotron, and Watts' Holst-inspired drum rolls at the climax are as unlikely and as joyous a moment as you'll find on the record.

ON WITH THE SHOW

After nine songs which exist somewhere between dream and the impending triumph of human space-travel, the real, sordid world of establishment night-clubs was invoked for a cathartic finale. Opening with a welcoming doorman ("there's a bar downstairs"), *verité* is maintained by MC Jagger, who, in pidgin-stiff-upper-lip, promises old-time favourites like 'Old Man River' and 'Stormy Weather', friendly dancers and hostesses, even a taxi for those too soaked to find their way home.

The inevitable descent arrived, with Nicky Hopkins' intoxicated cabaret-style piano (including a few bars of 'Chopsticks') and 'Harpo' Jones' crazed harp strumming attempting to keep up with the out-of-control rumba rhythm. It ends with Jagger under a table with a girl who hopes he "didn't record any of this": within months, he'd come to regret that he did, though since the early Seventies, he – and he alone among the band – has held a soft spot for the album.

Rolling Stones
Beggars Banquet

R.S.V.P.

Beggars Banquet
(LONDON 800 084-2 RELEASED DECEMBER 1968)

It's often been said that a mind unlocked by psychedelics is better equipped to perceive simple truths. It didn't always work – Pink Floyd's Syd Barrett and the Stones' own Brian Jones are good examples of the ever-restless post-acid mind – but after the technicolour dream came a quest for origins. The Beatles' cure for an LSD-induced hangover was a return to rock'n'roll for the Fifties-inspired 'Lady Madonna'; Bob Dylan re-emerged with an album of country songs.

'Beggars Banquet' was obviously conceived within this back-to-basics framework, but more than that, it was – after seven tries – their first really professional album. A 'proper' producer, Jimmy Miller (fresh from his work with The Spencer Davis Group and Traffic), was drafted in; distractions like tours, or the drug busts which interrupted the making of 'Satanic Majesties', were largely absent; songs were worked on prior to the sessions; and time, plus a grim determination to put the musical uncertainties of the past eighteen months behind them, all contributed to a new mood of optimism. "We were starting to find The Rolling Stones," said Keith Richards of 'Banquet'; and with Andrew Oldham out of the picture, and Brian Jones slowly but unquestionably fading, the Jagger/Richards partnership had become absolutely central to the quest.

Had the album's release not been delayed by some petty moral wrangling over the depiction of a graffitied lavatory wall on the cover, 'Banquet' probably would have enjoyed an even greater prominence. As it turned out, The Beatles' 'White Album' pipped it, and the Stones were once again accused of unduly shadowing the Fabs' every step. (This time, it was the stark white sleeve design, which was seen as a direct lift from The Beatles' album – in fact, the band had already considered a plain white sleeve a year earlier, for an abandoned 'We Love You' LP.)

There was one vital difference. The Beatles were already becoming less than the sum of their individual parts, whereas the Stones were reaching new heights of collective music-making. Even Brian Jones, increasingly a passenger on a journey of his own making, stayed upright long enough to contribute one or two wonderful touches. The band had even prepared for his unreliability, with pianist Nicky Hopkins joining midway through the sessions, and friends like Dave Mason and Eric Clapton occasionally dropping by at Olympic. Another visitor was leading French new wave film-maker Jean-Luc Godard, who shot footage of the band at work for his *One Plus One* film. Luck was on his side: he captured the dramatic unfolding of the opening track, 'Sympathy For The Devil'.

SYMPATHY FOR THE DEVIL

What Godard captured during his week-long stay with the Stones was the gradual development of this song from a slow, Dylan-styled ballad to a demonic samba beat, over which Jagger projected his Mephistophelean charms. So convincing was this exercise in public wish-fulfilment that the group lived in the song's shadow for the next decade, until someone realised that genuine Anti-Christs don't hob-nob with royalty or denounce punk rockers.

Marianne Faithfull recently described the song as "pure papier mâché Satanism", and she should know. Jagger's live-in lover at the time, she lent him Mikhail Bulgakov's *The Master And Margarita*, which provided the basis for the lyrics.

NO EXPECTATIONS

'Sympathy For The Devil' was hardly incomprehensible like much of 'Majesties', but neither was it exactly a return to more familiar musical ground. 'No Expectations' was, revealing Richards renewed passion for folk-blues. Based around the simplest of chord sequences, and drawing on the blues lyrically, with its themes of transience and on-the-hoof romance, it was left to Brian Jones to add the hauntingly authentic slide guitar lines. It was one of his last telling contributions to the Stones' music.

Note: the mono mix contained on the 'Singles Collection' box set is noticeably different.

Page 60

DEAR DOCTOR

Country music always lurked on the fringes of the Stones' repertoire: on 'Beggars Banquet' it was invited centre-stage. Keith Richards recalled that 'Dear Doctor' was "fun to play, almost a joke", because of the rhythm. Well, 3/4 wasn't *that* uncommon, though to the Stones, who played strictly four-four, it must have conjured up visions of ballrooms full of waltzing cowboys, as seen at the cinema in Saturday morning Westerns.

Jagger put on his best honky tonk voice as he recounted this parody of a li'l ol' country tale of a groom sick with doubt on his wedding day. There's even a happy ending when he discovers that his intended partner has run off to Virginia with his cousin.

PARACHUTE WOMAN

Although 'Beggars Banquet' was technically far superior to any previous band recording, Richards was fond of the process – first used on 'Jumpin' Jack Flash' – whereby the basic guitar and drum parts were first recorded on cassette. He'd then transfer this onto the Olympic eight-track. Consequently, after the other instrumentation, and vocals, had been added, the song would still retain a rough, mysterious aura. The subject matter on this song, which benefited from this technique, was similarly mischievous: the 'Parachute woman' was invited to "Land on me tonight", to "blow me out", and to "join me for a ride". Jagger's half of the bargain was to "break big in New Orleans" and "overspill in Caroline". Please allow me to introduce myself, but I'm a man with little regard for subtlety...

JIGSAW PUZZLE

Tramps, outcasts, perturbed Queens and grandmas who scream "Thanks!" on their deathbed: for the duration of this song, at least, Jagger really must have known how it felt to be Bob Dylan.

What was originally Mick's song had, by the time the band finished with it, become an epic, with Keith Richards enhancing the dreamscape with some eerie slide guitar, and Nicky Hopkins binding it together with his ornamental piano runs. The result was one of the band's few real masterpieces not powered by a single, memorable riff – which probably

explains why it's sometimes overlooked.

There's autobiography here, too, as Jagger sings (with uncharacteristic concern) of the angry singer, the shattered drummer, the guitar players, "damaged... outcasts all their lives" and, ahem, the bass player "nervous about the girls outside". Nervous?

STREET FIGHTING MAN

Jagger adopted several voices on 'Beggars Banquet': none, though, stuck as firmly as this battle cry, which railed at no-one in particular, and yet unwittingly provided the soundtrack to the riots in Paris, Chicago and Grosvenor Square. He attended the latter and, stirred by the experience, returned home to his Cheyne Walk residence to dash off some mixed-up observations. Others read it as inflammatory rhetoric, which was why some parts of the States banned the song.

The bare bones had been worked out long before Jagger decided to turn mass protest into poetry. The song began as 'Primo Grande', with Richards bashing out the riff on acoustic, accompanied by Watts on a toy drum kit, before some provisional lyrics

prompted a new title, 'Everybody Pays Their Dues', by which time many of the elements of the finished track were in place. It's still difficult to believe that Jagger's final lyrics, sung with all the urgency of an impending social catastrophe, were accompanied by a predominantly acoustic backing track. Rarely has rock conjured up a mood of impending violence with only a bass plugged in.

PRODIGAL SON
(Rev. Robert Wilkins)

The success of the Jagger/Richards partnership had effectively cut the Stones off from the music that initially inspired them. But, in preparation for this album, the band returned to their roots with jams based around Muddy Waters' 'Still A Fool' and Big Bill Broonzy's 'Rock Me Baby'. One country blues cover even made the finished album, this little-known version of Rev. Robert Wilkins' Biblical-charged 'Prodigal Son'.

As a reaction to the psychedelic excesses of yesteryear, Jagger had rediscovered his old Robert Johnson recordings, but it was Keith who found this one, spicing up with an open tuning favoured by the blues masters. Charlie Watts dusted off his brushes, Jagger turned in one of his best Dartford-on-the-Delta performances, and the result was one of the most dignified blues covers ever recorded by the band.

STRAY CAT BLUES

Fired up by the thought of 15-year-old girls demanding favours from the most lecherous rock'n'roll band on earth (caught, quite graphically, by artist Guy Peelaert, in his 'Rock Dreams' book), the Stones responded with this sexually-charged performance, macho to the point of obscenity. Couched in the symbolic form of the rock song, they got away with it, milking their full-bodied testosterone mystique for all it was worth.

Jagger later claimed that the song's tempo and malevolent sound derived from The Velvet Underground; certainly, the opening one-note guitar drone bore a close resemblance to that band's 'Heroin'. But on this occasion, the substance in question was destined to enter someone else's body, not their own. Cock rock, indeed.

FACTORY GIRL

Girls again, but this time not another on-the-road groupie story, but a genuine product of Jagger's imagination. The voice was pure deep south drawl, but the inspiration was more north of England, dark satanic mills chic.

Musically, though, it was all-American: Richards' impressive, hillbilly-like picking supplemented by Rick Grech's fiddle-playing and a mandolin.

SALT OF THE EARTH

Plucked from the anonymity of suburbia, the band had seen their lifestyles transformed beyond all recognition since 1963. But the example of their blues heroes, and of Bob Dylan, combined with the democratic instincts of the increasingly volatile Class of '68, prompted a second exercise in poverty chic. It was all rather unconvincing, even though the opening verse ("Let's drink to the hard-working people...") was croaked with some humility by Richards.

Jagger graciously exposed the fiction, invoking the "faceless crowds" who "don't look real to me, in fact they looked so

strange", an inbuilt expression of alienation from a community which he'd never really come to know.

To add to the cultural confusion, some gospel singers from Watts, Los Angeles, added the singalong chorus while the album was being mixed in the States, and while 'Salt Of The Earth' worked well as a climactic free-for-all for the finale of the still-unreleased *Rock'n'Roll Circus* TV special, the song never ventured out of the vaults again.

Let it Bleed

(LONDON 820 052-2, RELEASED DECEMBER 1969)

By the time 'Let It Bleed' appeared, in December 1969, it had virtually been eclipsed by the band's winter tour of the States. It was their biggest-grossing yet, and their first shows since pokey pop PAs had been replaced by the grand amplification systems of rock concerts. The greatest noise of all came from the highly charged atmosphere of a bitterly divided America. Campaigns against Vietnam, and racial and sexual inequality had intensified that year – and though the band were clearly on one side of the generational divide, the grand spectacle of the tour was increasingly cutting them off from their audiences. Against this background, the group organised the free concert at Altamont, an ill-fated show which ended in the kind of chaos and murder that many felt was synonymous with the Stones' music.

Like 'Beggars Banquet', 'Let It Bleed' opened with the sound of cultural catastrophe, but while 'Sympathy For The Devil' was Jagger in fantasy role-playing mode (albeit rather convincingly), 'Gimme Shelter' used no such distancing artistic device. No wonder the Maysles' brothers closed their film of the band's US tour with the song: after the death of Meredith Hunter, and the unrestrained violence which prevailed at the festival, which provided the film's climax, the song's apocalyptic scenario seemed to be uncannily prescient.

But until that moment, 'Let It Bleed',

recorded during the last months of 1968 and the first half of 1969, was more a collection of personal revelations than the grand socio-political anthems that some of the songs later became. If there is a locus for the album, then it's in the exclusive pockets of bohemia in Kensington and Chelsea.

Things had altered considerably since 'Beggars Banquet' provided the right cure for the psychedelic hangover. Brian Jones was sacked in May 1969, found dead in his swimming-pool on July 3, and ceremoniously exorcised at the open-air concert in Hyde Park two days later. And his replacement, Mick Taylor, a young protégé of John Mayall's blues-breaking school, had little chance to leave his imprint on the album. By 1969, the Stones centred on Mick and Marianne, Keith and Anita. Watts and Wyman remained loyal footservants, while exotic new courtiers, like Ry Cooder, Gram Parsons and Al Kooper were introduced into the inner circle for added musical muscle. The new Mark II edition of The Rolling Stones, which Keith had talked about at the 'Beggars' sessions, was finally falling into place, establishing unspoken ground-rules which, twenty-five years later, still dictate the band's working practices.

Yet, despite its origins, there is no real fear in the song. Although essentially a Keith Richards' composition (a version exists with him on vocals), Jagger's rapturous delivery transforms the scenario – storms, fires, floods, rape, war, murder – into one of pure voyeurism. Musically, the song is every bit as brutal, with Richards' multi-tracked guitars brooding and overly distorted, and Watts' heavily accentuated rhythm emphasising the 'shots' in the chorus. Best of all, though, is Merry Clayton, who duets with Jagger for much of the song, bringing out the song's spiritual associations with her full-bodied, soar-away gospel hollering.

GIMME SHELTER

Like 'Beggars Banquet', 'Let It Bleed' opened ominously, only this time, there was none of Jagger's devilish role-playing to distance the oppressive mood of a world balanced on an apocalyptic precipice. Altamont, Charles Manson, Kent State, all these events gave new meanings to a song which probably began life in the persecution-crazy months during 1967, when the band's only shelter was the recording studio.

LOVE IN VAIN
(Woody Payne)

For years, just one album's worth of Robert Johnson material was thought to exist. Then, around 1967-68, a second collection began to circulate, reawakening Jagger and Richards' interest in the Delta blues. One of these newly-unearthed titles was 'Love In Vain', which the pair felt compelled to cover. "It was just so beautiful: the title, the lyrics, the ideas, the rhymes, just everything about it," recalled Richards.

The note-for-note evangelical purism of six or seven years ago was long gone: instead, the pair opted for a more countrified approach, with Keith's slide and Ry Cooder's mandolin-playing capturing something of Johnson's haunting style. Although performed in rehearsal at the *Rock And Roll Circus* in December 1968, the song was first properly premièred at the Hyde Park concert in 1969, a fitting tribute to the band's own transient Johnson fan who too had "left the station".

COUNTRY HONK

"That's how I wrote it," recalled Richards, "as a real Hank Williams/Jimmie Rodgers/Thirties country song. And it got turned around to this other thing by Mick Taylor who got into a completely different feel throwing it off the wall another way."

Byron Bertine's fiddle brings out the Williams associations (Hank's 'Honky Tonk Blues' provides the model), Nanette Newman plays bar-room queen to Jagger's mock-Southern leer, while the rest of the world got an insight into Mick Taylor's immediate effect on the band, by comparing it with 'Honky Tonk Women'.

LIVE WITH ME

By the time the band had laid down the basis of this song in London, then called in tenor sax player Bobby Keyes and Leon Russell whom they met in Los Angeles while mixing the album, 'Live With Me' became one of their scrappiest arrangements since the 'Satanic Majesties' days.

Still, the lengthy association with Keyes, whom they'd first encountered playing with Bobby Vee's band in San Antonio in June 1964, made it all worthwhile. As the version on 'Get Yer Ya-Ya's Out!' showed, the song worked better live.

LET IT BLEED

The first Stones' song to translate into an album title, 'Let It Bleed' lays bare Mick's easily-detectable word-games (Marianne Faithfull verifies the "parking-lot"/vagina metaphor in her recent autobiography), and Keith's increasingly fluid slide guitar playing, prompted by his continued association with ex-Byrds guitarist and passionate country music fiend Gram Parsons. Sandwiched in between are images of self-satisfied decadence and an effective use of one of the most familiar chord patterns in rock. The song is also notable for welcoming pianist Ian Stewart back into the fold: with Nicky Hopkins almost always on hand, Stu only managed this one performance on the album.

MIDNIGHT RAMBLER

Like 'Live With Me', this studio recording of 'Midnight Rambler' bears little comparison with the live version on 'Ya-Ya's'. Lacking the powerful Richards/Taylor interplay, it only hints at the blood-curdling *tour de force* it would become in concert, complete with Jagger's sadistic stage-whipping.

At face value, it's another glorification of contemporary evil – this time the notorious murderer Edward DeSalvo, already mythologised as the Boston Strangler. But it runs deeper than that, its dark mood, and surprisingly subtle twists gave it the aura of a long-lost tributary from the Mississippi swampland. Jagger's harp-playing was particularly impressive, though Jones' credit for percussion has long mystified fans: perhaps it was simply a gesture of affection to the man who'd long felt the band had betrayed the blues roots.

Any subtleties were soon extinguished when the band readied the song for the US '69 tour, and almost immediately, 'Midnight Rambler' formed the centrepiece of the Stones' live show for several years. And just to show that not everyone takes rock'n'roll symbolism seriously, sections of the audience (male and female) would punctuate the song's rape/murder scene with ecstatic, agonised, screams.

YOU GOT THE SILVER

Keith Richards' first complete solo vocal performance on a Stones' record, 'You Got The Silver' was this love song written for his girlfriend Anita Pallenberg in 1968. Beautifully executed, it was one of the final recordings to feature Brian Jones (autoharp) and Richards (acoustic and slide guitars) working together. A version exists with Jagger on vocals, but while technically weaker, Richards' rendition wins hands down for sheer depth of feeling.

MONKEY MAN

Long forgotten, this song has recently been unearthed for the band's recent tour, perhaps because Ron Wood believes it features one of Riffmeister Richards' finest ever guitar licks. He might be right, too, the only thing letting the song down being a distinct lack of a similarly gutsy vocal hook, and some truly throwaway lyrics. Nicky Hopkins presages some of his wonderful piano work on 'Exile On Main St.', while Jimmy Miller gets a fine, tub-thumping performance out of Charlie. Good tonight, good most nights.

YOU CAN'T ALWAYS GET WHAT YOU WANT

Once upon a time, the Stones accentuated their frustration songs with a fuzz box and an unusual, near-spoken vocal delivery. By 1969, they'd recruited the 50-piece London Bach Choir to ram the message home. What that message meant, of course, was always open to question: the death of Sixties idealism? A new blueprint for Seventies realism? Or, as Marianne Faithfull has it, "It was about my romance with drugs."

The basis of the song (which was basically Jagger's) was taped at an all-night session in November 1968: Al Kooper played the organ and, notes Bill Wyman, Brian Jones lay on his back all night stoned out of his head while reading an article about botany. Although performed at the *Rock And Roll Circus* TV special, the dramatic arrangements came later, with Jack Nitzsche arranging the massed vocals in May 1969.

Part Two

The Atlantic Years 1971-1977

The Relationship between their singles and albums, which were mutually exclusive throughout the Sixties, altered after the Stones formed their own Rolling Stones record label in conjunction with Atlantic. The new practice was to preview each new album with a single, and that policy was maintained throughout these years.

The rights to the 1971-77 material has since followed the Stones from Atlantic to EMI, CBS and more recently, to Virgin. There are CBS CDs around, but the advice is not to bother with them: Virgin has handled the catalogue splendidly, issuing all the original Atlantic titles in June 1994 in special 'collectors' editions'. These boasted miniaturised facsimiles of the original artwork – postcards, inserts, gatefolds, die-cut sleeves, even the 'Sticky Fingers' zipper – as well as superbly remastered sound. Sadly, these were in limited supply, ranging from 115,000 copies of 'It's Only Rock'n'Roll' to 202,000 copies of 'Sticky Fingers

Sticky Fingers

(VIRGIN 7243-8-39504-2-3, RELEASED APRIL 1971)

Expensive and gimmicky record sleeves often mask a paucity of ideas inside. That wasn't the case with the keenly-awaited 'Sticky Fingers', which welcomed the world with an Andy Warhol-designed cover of a jean-clad male crotch, complete with zipper. After all, it heralded a series of firsts: first studio set of the new decade; first on their new, apparently self-run label (actually, Rolling Stones Records was largely a triumph of marketing); first with Mick Taylor firmly in place as second guitarist; first since the band had taken off to the South of France (for tax avoidance purposes); and, quite important this, the first since Jagger confirmed his arrival with the jet-set via his much-publicised romance with, and subsequent marriage to, Bianca-with-the-unpronounceable surname.

Hard-nosed business deals, and a lifestyle where expensive diamonds and almost as expensive drug-deals appeared to be every-day occurrences, seemed a far cry from the interminable round of concert tours and hasty studio sessions endured throughout the Sixties. The band earned a lot of money during its early years, but had seemingly little control over their financial affairs. With their Decca deal running out at the end of July 1970, they decided to reappraise the situation.

Against this background, which was to set the tone for the entire decade – get wise, move on up, but keep on skinning up – the Stones were able to fulfil their self-declared 'greatest rock'n'roll band in the world' status with consummate ease. As the counter-culture crumbled around them (Jones, Jimi and Janis were dead, The Beatles strangled by a web of law-suits, and idealistic hippies wilted into drug-addled hairies), the band managed to epitomise the new dispirited age without actually becoming part of its fall-out.

Music wasn't, after all, about to change the world. Jagger had said as much on 'Street Fighting Man' and, more obliquely, 'You Can't

Always Get What You Want'. 'Sticky Fingers' interiorised this, matching it with an attention to detail hitherto unknown in their previous work. What price the revolution when Taylor and Richards were coming up with the kind of organic interplay the band had only dreamed about during the Jones' era? What value all those interminable debates when an ironic celebration of the band's milieu was within Jagger's grasp? And who'd take the doomy predictions for rock's future seriously after this, the Stones' first truly timeless long-player?

BROWN SUGAR

The buzzing intro of 'Satisfaction' may define its era more instantly, but it's the overly distorted opening chords of 'Brown Sugar' which more accurately demonstrate the classic Stones sound. Thankfully, none of the scuzziness has been lost on the laudable CD transfers effected by new licensees Virgin in 1994, although over-familiarity has probably blunted the impact of the lyrics, which cannot be read in any way other than as a parody of colonial and misogynist values. What can a not-so-poor boy do 'cept lampoon his own cock-thrusting, white bluesman self?

Recorded in Muscle Shoals, Alabama, back in December 1969, 'Brown Sugar' lay dormant for almost eighteen months. Had a single been delayed so long in the mid-Sixties, it would have been discarded, rendered obsolete by the technical and compositional advances which transformed pop on an almost weekly basis. There was talk of substituting a second version taped at Olympic on Keith Richards' birthday a year later, with Eric Clapton on slide and Al Kooper on keyboards, but happily sense prevailed over novelty.

The bonus track on the 'Brown Sugar' maxi-single was a rip-roaring version of Chuck Berry's 'Let It Rock', recorded live at Leeds University on 13 March 1971.

SWAY

If there's a moment that encapsulates everything that's wonderful about the album, then it might well be Jagger's fatigued "1-2-3-4" intro on this underrated number, forever kept in the shadow by its predecessor. Procrastination was increasingly becoming the order of the day for 'serious' musicians: but this rehearsal group homily set up an agonising sense of expectation quite out of character for its time. Remember, this was the period when wild-haired baton-swinging renegades from the world of classical music were being called upon to elevate rock into High Art.

Strings were used sparingly on the track – , courtesy of arranger Paul Buckmaster – but 'Sway' (an intriguing, non-Stones-like title, too) was more death-rattle than rattle-your-jewellery finery.

WILD HORSES

The final nail in that "If it ain't blues, it ain't got no feeling" jive the Stones used to spin to their predominantly white, overwhelmingly pop audiences. Actually, on 'Wild Horses', the band had merely made explicit another strain in their heritage – country music – but rather than take the easier, tongue-in-cheek mimicry of, say, 'Dear Doctor', they stepped inside the genre and turned in something uniquely their own.

The influence of Gram Parsons was plainly evident, and it was his Flying Burrito Brothers who first released the song in Spring 1970. But, replete with those Marianne Faithfull associations (the repeated refrain of 'Wild Horses couldn't drag me away' was, she insists, her first words to Jagger as she pulled out of a coma after overdosing in 1969), the song has since entered the premier league of Stones' self-mythologising songs. No matter that Keith maintains that he wrote the chorus in the toilet at Muscle Shoals: "It was about Marlon's birth," he said, "because I knew we were going to have to go to America and start work again... and (I was) not really wanting to go away."

CAN'T YOU HEAR ME KNOCKING

Someone in the Stones' camp had been listening to Santana, the West Coast ensemble with a heavy emphasis on Latin beats and sprightly percussion. In spite of the song being dominated by a lengthy instrumental passage (featuring Jimmy Miller, Rocky Dijon on percussion, organist Billy Preston, and sax player Bobby Keyes sparring with a lengthy guitar solo), Ronnie Wood has since reclaimed the song for Keith Richards' maddeningly effective opening riff; Jagger literally so when he performed it on his 1988 Australian solo tour.

YOU GOTTA MOVE
(Fred McDowall)

Another song dating from the winter '69 Muscle Shoals sessions, this completed a trilogy of Delta blues covers on successive albums. 'Elmo' Taylor's slide playing darted in and out of the slow, worksong backing, though Jagger's best Library of Congress recording series voice probably wouldn't have convinced folk-blues chronicler Alan Lomax. The song became a concert favourite throughout the Seventies.

BITCH

Sometimes, critics write off Keith Richards' Chuck Berry impressions as if they don't really matter. The riffs might be as familiar as a Coca-Cola trademark, but as Andy Warhol tried to show with his Campbell's soup can screenprints, ubiquity need not compromise beauty.

'Bitch' was first-class braggadocio, with Jagger milking his stoned stud persona for all its worth (an obvious response, one figures, to Marianne Faithfull's decision to end their affair), but the brassy, macho urgency counts for nothing when it's disrupted by Richards' masterful

break. From that moment, the rock'n'rolling clichés were *all* that made the song matter.

I GOT THE BLUES

This carefully paced album continued with what's little more than a musical tribute to the men who gave the band its start in pop-life. Bobby Keyes and Jim Price do their best Stax horns impression, Billy Preston plays a solemn gospel organ, while Jagger gets inside the measured pace with no mean conviction.

SISTER MORPHINE

For six months, this Jagger song existed purely as an A minor chord with a decorative seventh thrown in. By the time Marianne Faithfull had added the full weight of her pain (displaced, as she maintains the song was about a fictional character on his deathbed after a car accident), Ry Cooder added some tremendous bottleneck playing, and the band concocted some of the most subtle dynamics they'd ever laid down in the studio, it had become one of their most accomplished works.

Marianne had recorded it first, while the band were finishing 'Let It Bleed', but the nature of the song wasn't to Decca's liking and it was quickly withdrawn. It's since become, in her words, her "Frankenstein" – which in time consumed her, destroyed her recording career and compelled her to do battle with conflicting wills ever since.

DEAD FLOWERS

This uptempo country rocker, with tongue firmly in cheek, was one of the album's weaker moments, made slightly less tolerable by its juvenile display of drug chic: "I'll be in my basement room, with a needle and a spoon". Jagger goes some way to make amends with some hilarious Tennessee Williams-speak, "making bets on Kentuck-ee Durr-bee Day-ee", which probably amuses Jerry Hall no end.

MOONLIGHT MILE

Here's ample proof that the musical hub of the Stones isn't always Keith Richards. 'Moonlight Mile' was Jagger's epic soliloquy on America – a chilling evocation of a vast expanse which, after years of familiarity, still seemed an irrepressible and essentially untameable land. No doubt inspired by the strain of lengthy tours there, Huckleberry Jagger can hear only meaningless talk in the voices of strangers, and silence on his radio. Weary and resigned, he calls in Paul Buckmaster to finish the song off with an all-encompassing string arrangement. Mick Taylor thought that he deserved a writing co-credit on the song.

Exile On Main St.
(VIRGIN 7243-8-39503-2-4, MAY 1972)

Study a handful of rock magazines and you'll soon discover that every third musician is described as a 'legend', and every band has turned in 'one of the greatest rock albums of all time'. The nature of the game is, after all, not puzzling but hyperbole. But if critical opinion is anything to go by, 'Exile' – which, as some might remember, was greeted with a mixed press on its release – has emerged as one of the most complete rock double albums ever released.

The excuse for 'Satanic Majesties' is, rightly or wrongly, usually cited as the undue pressure of court cases and an excess of drugs clouding the creative juices. A better explanation is probably an excess of contemporary musical fashion. In fact, the Stones work better when under pressure to deliver and, while far from starving artists working alone in an unwelcome world, their isolation in Keith's villa in the South of France, combined with unsettled financial affairs and a front-man whose main concern appeared to be nursing his pregnant wife, were all factors which conspired to make 'Exile' what it is. In fact, the newly-married Jagger, out to prove that he hadn't completely made his peace with conventional mores, turned in some of the best performances of his career.

What makes 'Exile' so special? The album contained no era-defining songs like 'You Can't Always Get What You Want' or 'Sympathy For The Devil', nor any introspective epics like 'Moonlight Mile', or showy assertions of their satanic majesty, like 'Midnight Rambler'. No individual song is remembered as the high-point, nor did the album in any way encapsulate the prevailing mood. With glam rock and progressive rock and singer-songwriters in the ascendant, it's perhaps little wonder that it was greeted with a hum and a ho first time round.

What 'Exile' captured was a band wholly conversant with their own limitations. By defining their own terms, and by not falling foul of contemporary fads and fashions, the Stones touched base with what inspired them in the first place. The act of collective music-making, in the leisured ambience of a kitchen/basement, enabled them to fulfil what they weren't able to achieve back in 1962. And now able to draw on all the sources they'd accessed during their ten-year career, their vast musical education enabled them to fully control those influences, rather than let themselves simply become the sum of them.

There's nothing ostentatious, or even immediately gripping about the results. But rarely has a group reacquainted itself with both the original, and a contemporary vision of itself, and emerged with a hybrid that seemed quintessential, and yet wonderfully out-of-sorts with both. Welcome to Main Street.

but the sheer inability to decipher the words contributed to rock'n'roll's mystique. It was advice that Jagger never forgot. The production on the Stones' early records, in particular, was often derided for its sheer incomprehensibility, but rather than incompetence on the part of producer Andrew Oldham, it was as much a wilful exercise in obfuscation. And never was it put to better use than on this record.

Ostensibly a bar-room rocker, 'Rocks Off' was probably closer to The Velvet Underground's 'White Light/White Heat', both in its unadulterated onslaught of sound, and in its speed-driven, brain-addled reportage. Jagger being Jagger, the sexual overtones were explicit, though who understood – on first hearing, at least – the underlying fear of impending impotence?

ROCKS OFF

Fats Domino has never been acknowledged as a primary influence on the band. Yet an impressionable young Jagger was struck by a quote of his concerning diction and the contemporary popular voice. Fats believed that it wasn't necessary to sing the lyrics clearly: not only was the content secondary to the sound,

RIP THIS JOINT

That the Stones took this set of songs out on the road to vast American stadiums was little short of criminal: 'Rip This Joint' was built for clubland, the audience showered by spit from Bobby Keyes' blistering sax, the floor caving in with the crush of bodies whipped into a frenzy by two minutes of classic rock'n'roll.

With Stu bashing out the piano keys and Bill Plummer testing the limits of his thick-stringed double bass, this – not Janov's – was the primal therapy Lennon really desired.

SHAKE YOUR HIPS
(James Moore)

Jagger's Slim Harpo impression was real enough to conjure up images of one of those weird Southern boys propping up a bar in Memphis. Thankfully, no eye contact was required here.

Like the band's take on Willie Dixon's 'I Just Want To Make Love To You', their version of 'Shake Your Hips' (alias 'Hip Shake') was handled well without falling into parody or sophisticated, whited-out blandness. How the Stones completely lost the knack of doing this in the years ahead is something they probably don't even understand themselves.

Apparently, this track was taped as early as October 1970, at Olympic Studios, although it was later reworked at Keith's Château Nellcôte, pleasingly located in Villefranche Sur Mer, midway between Nice and Monte Carlo on the French Riviera.

CASINO BOOGIE

Not one of the album highlights, 'Casino Boogie' (it sounds like its title suggests it might) is saved by Bobby Keyes' artful sax break and the fact that lines like "Dietrich movies, close up boogies" are incomprehensible without the aid of the sheet music.

TUMBLING DICE

This started life as 'Good Time Woman', with a completely different set of lyrics ("Red light woman sure like to party", etc.). Not for the first time on the album, Mick Taylor handled the bass duties, while Jagger's down-on-women line was tempered by the amusing aside that he was "all sixes and sevens and nines". Clydie King and Vanetta Fields provided the most effective backing vocals on a Stones' single to date, and it was one of the most unassuming, too. But there was little else on the album that would have done the job better: 'Exile' was nothing if not a set of brilliantly-executed half-singles.

SWEET VIRGINIA

The nearest the Stones ever got to a round-the-campfire song, though Baden-Powell probably wouldn't have appreciated the refrain. "Got to scrape the shit right off your shoes" suggested that the song may have been an obscure slant on the old standard 'Walking Blues', but the blues (and the reds and the greens, for that matter) referred to in the song were in tablet form. If one Stones' song was written by Keith and Gram Parsons up in the Blue Ridge Mountains, 'Sweet Virginia' must have been it.

SWEET BLACK ANGEL

Even the Black and White Minstrels might have hesitated over a line like "Ten liddle nigga, sittin' on deh wall", but Jagger's wildly exaggerated delivery of a tender message of support to black American radical Angela Davis (She's a sweet black angel/not a gun totin' teacher/not a Red lovin' school mom") barely raised an eyelid. There is something distinctly odd about Jagger's most outrageous act of mimicry yet (not to mention the exotic, jungle-evoking backing) as he delivered the "free de sweet black slave" punchline, but the sentiments sideswept the almost painful parody.

TORN AND FRAYED

The "restless" guitar player, with his coat T&F'd, and his friends wondering "who's gonna help him to kick it", suggest a rare pen-portrait of Keith from the inside. But the "ballrooms and smelly bordellos"? The band "a bag of nerves on first nights"? Surely not. What could have been a throwaway was elevated by some splendid steel guitar, courtesy of Al Perkins, atmospheric organ from horn player Jim Price, and Jagger providing just the right featherlight touch the song required.

LOVING CUP

First recorded in spring 1969, and premiered at the July '69 Hyde Park concert, 'Loving Cup' had a long gestation period. With Nicky Hopkins and a punchy brass section in tow, the Stones furthered their own white gospel ambitions in tub-thumping fashion, a good way short of the plunge into caricature. That, in a few words, is what 'Exile' is all about: a pivotal moment where they retained perfect control of their influences and their own destiny. They wouldn't always make it look so easy in the years ahead.

THE ATLANTIC YEARS 1971-1977 : EXILE ON MAIN ST.

HAPPY

Almost entirely of Richards' making – he wrote the song, played guitar and bass, and even provided the template for his future lead vocal sorties – 'Happy', was basically cut as a warm-up. Hence the impromptu backing group of just Jimmy Miller on drums and Bobby Keyes on sax. Jagger helped guide the melody at a later date, but essentially it's Keith's show.

TURD ON THE RUN

With instrumental backing very much the out-raged offspring of 'Stoned' almost a decade ear-lier, 'Turd On The Run' belied its jokey title, pro-viding just the mood of uptightness that Jagger revels in. He blew a pretty vitriolic harp, too.

VENTILATOR BLUES
(Jagger/Richards/Mick Taylor)

So close to somnambulance and yet so far. It was a measure of the band's greatness during this period that they could walk the line marked turgid and transform a grizzly riff into something invested with all the 'soul' they'd once sought to locate in second-rate covers of Otis Redding songs. 'Ventilator Blues' was white boy spit'n'sawdust blues at its best, and the Mick Taylor co-credit his first.

I JUST WANT TO SEE HIS FACE

Had 'Exile' not been spread over four sides, the band probably would have played safe and songs like this Dr. John-influenced voodoo incantation would probably not have made the grade. Thankfully, it was, for it's in the album's margins that its true greatness lies.

LET IT LOOSE

If the band's early excursions into gospel were tentative and sometimes painfully self-conscious, all doubts had been cast away by 1971. Up to half-a-dozen backing singers joined Jagger in a rare display of genuine emotion (well that's what it sounded like: don't study the lyrics too closely), while the horn arrangements were all but Memphis in name.

ALL DOWN THE LINE

'All Down The Line' preceded the main body of 'Exile' sessions by a good eighteen months, having first been recorded in October 1969 at Elektra Studios, Los Angeles. At one stage, this top-rate rocker was tipped as the band's first post-Decca 45, but 'Brown Sugar' proved to be insurmountable opposition. It eventually surfaced on 7" in America as the follow-up to 'Tumbling Dice'.

STOP BREAKING DOWN

(Traditional, arranged
Jagger/Richards/Wyman/Taylor/Watts)

Learnt from the Robert Johnson version, originally recorded in 1937, this was exactly the kind of song Brian Jones wanted the band to make during the 'Beggars Banquet' sessions. They didn't, but two years later, Mick Taylor was on hand to turn in some measured slide guitar. The basics were recorded at Olympic between 17-31 October 1970, with Jagger adding his ever-improving harp playing at a later date.

SHINE A LIGHT

Another song originally laid down at the October 1970 Olympic sessions, 'Shine A Light' begins deceptively with a flashback of electronically-generated psychedelic sound, before Jagger sermonises to the sound of Billy Preston's hotline-to-heaven organ-playing.

There was more than a hint of camp in his voice (the dropping of the 'r's, for instance), but the overall effect was more successful than 'Salt Of The Earth' ever was. And the band weren't afraid to experiment, as the highly echoed guitar, and an 'underwater effect' on the backing vocals, amply illustrate.

SOUL SURVIVOR

Typically evasive in his meaning, Jagger's 'Soul Survivor' ("gonna be the death of me") provides a fitting end to the Stones' finest hour (give or take seven minutes). A savage reassertion, not of the soul and gospel influences that soaked much of 'Exile', but of their immediately recognisable hard rock style, the song captures the band at their best: getting the most out of a riff, verses that shy clear of melodic flamboyance and a deceptively

rousing non-chorus.

It's a pity the song never entered the band's regular concert repertoire. It wasn't conventionally crowd-pleasing (it's difficult to imagine Wembley Stadium clapping along as one to its jagged riff), though lack of exposure has frozen it in time. It's one of the last truly awesome expressions of the Stones' greatness – when they managed to make the instantly familiar sound like it had just been invented.

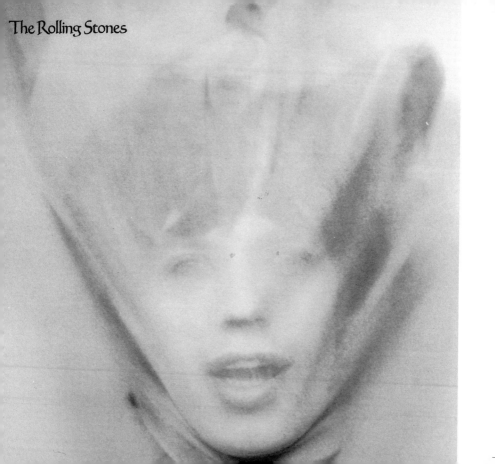

Goats Head Soup

(VIRGIN 7243-8-39498-2-3, RELEASED AUGUST 1973)

Keith Richards later described 'Goats Head Soup' as "a marking time album", a view that's widely shared among even the most enthusiastic Stones' watchers. That wasn't the plan as the band jetted off to Byron Lee's Dynamic Sound Studios, in Kingston, Jamaica, for some intense pre-Christmas sessions toward the end of 1972.

The decision to record in Jamaica was inspired by the band's romantic attachment to black music, on this occasion the emerging reggae sounds. They got there early – Island Records didn't begin to push Bob Marley until the following year – but they also got it wrong. Reggae's greatest contribution to popular music was its pioneering use of the recording studio as an auxiliary instrument. With producer Jimmy Miller and engineer Andy Johns in tow, the Stones brought too many safety valves along with them. They went to Jamaica to witness the new techniques at first hand, but first and foremost to use a high-tech studio. Had they linked up with veteran producer Lee Perry, 'Goats Head Soup' would have turned out quite differently, and the band might not have plunged so quickly into self-

parody. That wasn't the whole of the story – indeed, there is much on 'Soup' which defies its low-key reputation – but the affair smacks of a good chance wasted.

DANCING WITH MR D

The tone of the album was clearly set by this mildly soporific revival of that ole black magic theme. The sound was suitably dank, the air probably did smell sweet, but the song was certainly no match for 'Sympathy For The Devil'. Instead, the hook – an inverse of the 'Jumpin' Jack Flash' riff – was too self-conscious to resonate with the kind of satanic majesty it required. Perhaps that was the desired effect, a complete debunking of the diabolic mythology that had surrounded the band for the past five years. Even so, it hardly did the band any favours.

100 YEARS AGO

The clavinet was fast-becoming the hippest instrument in American black music, and old friend Billy Preston was on hand to lend his expertise in that department. The song probably didn't start out that way, as it's rumoured to have been first aired at the 'Exile' sessions. The funk hit hardest when, towards the end of the song, Mick Taylor took off on a heavily wah-wahed solo, elevating a perfunctory exercise in contemporary fashion into something that stepped aside, and looked beyond.

DOO DOO DOO DOO DOO (HEARTBREAKER)

'Heartbreaker' was uptempo and brassy enough to be one of the few new songs the band took out with them on their 1973 European tour. Always keen to keep up with social, as well as musical trends, the Stones drew on the collective nightmares of urban America – an innocent boy shot by the cops, a ten-year-old girl sticking needles in her arm – and couched them in the breathlessly excited manner of a 'Mystery Movie' soundtrack.

COMING DOWN AGAIN

The combination of some characteristic delicacy on the part of pianist Nicky Hopkins, and Keith's languid wah-wah rhythm (played through a Leslie speaker for added effect) provides a perfect counterpoint to 'Happy' on 'Exile'. Always less verbose than Jagger, Richards preferred method for announcing a sexual peccadillo to the world was to bathe in its sensuality, as opposed to Jagger's more macho response. Bobby Keyes' sax break towards the end only served to enhance the sumptuous, carefree aura.

ANGIE

Who was 'Angie'? Some took the obvious inference that it must have been the wife of Jagger's new playmate David Bowie, but that was just lazy journalism. The sad eyes, the dreams that all went up in smoke – and even the David Bailey photograph on the album cover, featuring a shrouded Jagger uncannily resembling his ex-beau – all pointed to Marianne Faithfull, though that went little remarked upon at the time.

Largely forgotten amidst the identification crisis was the fact that the band had stylishly revisited the tender acoustic ballads which once formed a notable part of their repertoire. A sharp contrast with their usual ballsy single material, 'Angie' solicited compliments from unlikely sources, yet it polarised their long-term disciples. There was no danger in Hopkins' sensitive playing, nor in Nick Harrison's string arrangements, it's true, but it was always their audience, and not the band themselves who'd set the band up as the first battalion of the counter-culture. What could be more dangerous than to puncture people's perceptions once in a while?

SILVER TRAIN

Trains, Mick Taylor on slide guitar, some earthy harp-playing and Ian Stewart back on the piano stool – the blues were back in fashion, at least for one song. American bluesman Johnny Winter got wind of 'Silver Train' early on, and beat the Stones to it by issuing his own hard-rock version on 'Still Alive And Well' in March 1973. Had it appeared on 'Exile', it might have enjoyed a better reputation, but here, it sounded rather lost and perfunctory. It gave Jagger a good excuse for his customary finger-pointing, mouth puckering and strutting on the 1973 tour, though.

HIDE YOUR LOVE

While Jagger and Richards once began songs together, on 'Soup' the separation between their work was far more apparent than before. The days of popping round to one another's home studios in Cheyne Walk were gone, and it's likely that Jagger presented 'Hide Your Love', fumbling staccato piano-playing'n'all, at the session as a *fait accompli*. Had Bill Wyman written it, the song probably wouldn't have got a look-in.

WINTER

Jagger as Earth Father? It seemed an unlikely guise for the man who'd just been filmed delighting in laddish abandon of the rock'n'roll roadshow for Robert Frank's *Cocksucker Blues* documentary of the 1972 US tour. Yet he almost pulled it off, with this almost filmic version of grand old country themes like hardship and longing. Nicky Hopkins and Nick Harrison gave the song added grandeur, but ultimately it failed to develop into something more than its opening theme suggested.

CAN YOU HEAR THE MUSIC

Eastern bells, flutes and percussion were essentially psychedelic rock ingredients, so what were they doing here, five years on? The lyrics, too, suggested that it was something of a flashback, with "magic floating in the air", rainbows and plenty of mystery. Even the title was chanted, mantra-style.

STAR STAR

Banned by the BBC, remixed in the States to mask the word "pussy", and the subject of considerable debate in the offices of the Stones' paymasters Atlantic Records, who declined to go ahead with the song under its original title, 'Starfucker'. It all made good copy for the world's newsdesks, but the song was little more than vaudeville, one of their least convincing Chuck Berry stylisations, with some mildly amusing lyrics obviously inspired by on-tour high-jinks. The line about "giving head to Steve McQueen" rather tickled the actor, I'm reliably informed.

It's Only Rock'n'Roll

(VIRGIN 7243-8-39500-2-7, RELEASED OCTOBER 1974)

If 'Goats Head Soup' was an overly-sophisticated response to the DIY production on 'Exile', then this time round, they chose to take destiny in their own hands. Ending their fruitful, five-year relationship with producer Jimmy Miller, Jagger and Richards re-styled themselves The Glimmer Twins (a pseudonym dating back to a winter '68 trip to Rio). With the assistance of engineers Andy Johns and Keith Harwood, the band entered the Musicland Studios in Munich during November 1973, returning for further sessions the following January, to reclaim their exalted status.

The results may have banished the memories of the subdued 'Soup' album, but it's difficult to make a case for 'It's Only Rock'n'Roll' as the true inheritor to 'Exile On Main St.'. The Guy Peelaert-designed sleeve said it all: glam rock had redefined pop on Hollywood lines, and Peelaert's depiction of the band making a grand entrance onto a set of Cecil B. de Mille-like proportions neatly encapsulated not only their own rank in the rock'n'roll pecking order, but also rock's increasing tendency towards grandiose spectacle.

The Hollywood invoked by Bolan and Bowie bore all the arcane mystery of the Silent Age, sexually ambiguous and not easily penetrable.

The Stones instead opted for the star-studded epic, tailored towards easy mass consumption and with the simplest of story-lines: "It's only rock'n'roll but I like it". Well, nice to see you, to see you nice, and all that, but the album marked the band's decisive entry into a comfortable living as rock's elder statesmen. From this point on, their youth cultural importance vanished (though the much-publicised graffiti campaign to promote the album tried – a little too hard, it must be said – to dress the record up in contemporary street-cred), and there would be few musical surprises in the future. On 'It's Only Rock'n'Roll', the band had become what they imagined their mass audience desired them to be. They were wrong.

IF YOU CAN'T ROCK ME

The ingredients were there – curt riff, solid backing, and a Jagger vocal that was buried within, as opposed to above, the sound – but 'If You Can't Rock Me' never really threatened 'Brown Sugar' or 'Rocks Off'. A chance to elevate the song into something more than simply coasting was missed during the un-inspired instrumental break, while Jagger's playful, self-referential lyrics were distinctly unmemorable. The line, "I think I better just sing one more song," was telling, for this sounded like the band were back in the studio for reasons of necessity not passion.

AIN'T TOO PROUD TO BEG
(Norman Whitfield/Eddie Holland)

Two covers were recorded during the ses-sions, Dobie Gray's 'Drift Away', and this version of an old Temptations US hit from 1966. It's most memorable for a brief Keith Richards solo, a triumph of pent-up economy which contrasted with the rest of the song. Apart from that, it could have been any bunch of old-timers with some studio time and a handful of Motown 45s for inspiration.

IT'S ONLY ROCK'N'ROLL (BUT I LIKE IT)

"It was Mick and Keith trying to write some-thing in the classic Stones style," remem-bered Mick Taylor, implying that the end result wasn't really up to scratch. Actually, the song began life in Ron Wood's Richmond home studio in the summer of '73, just prior to the band's European tour. Keith wasn't around, so the original demo featured Jagger and Wood on guitars, Willie Weeks on bass, and Faces' drummer Kenney Jones. Mick took that version to Munich, Richards liked what he heard, and built the rest of the song around it.

'It's Only Rock'n'Roll' (like Ian Dury's 'Sex & Drugs & Rock'n'Roll') is a cliché first, and then a song, but despite its almost crass conviviality, spare an ear for Richards' grainy Chuck Berry-isms, which raised the tone considerably. Sounding every bit like the superstar jam session it once was, the song remains a stage favourite, and has some historical importance in that it was the first evidence of Ronnie Wood's slow move into the centre of the Stones' orbit. Lost over time, though, was its obvious lyrical debt to Bowie's 'Rock'n'Roll Suicide'.

The single was backed by 'Through The Lonely Nights', a slow Jagger/Richards ballad rumoured to feature Jimmy Page on guitar. This was a left-over from the 'Goats Head Soup' sessions.

TILL THE NEXT GOODBYE

Nicky Hopkins and Mick Taylor excelled on the ornamental acoustic-based numbers on 'Sticky Fingers', and it was to songs like 'Wild Horses' which 'Till The Next Goodbye' looked for inspiration. Some nice snatches of slide guitar, an accomplished, leisurely performance from Charlie Watts, and some attractive acoustic guitar wasn't enough to guarantee the song any future other than offering an interlude after the most high-spirited start to a Stones' album for several years.

TIME WAITS FOR NO ONE

Jagger has Mick Taylor to thank for providing a notable distraction to some of his most pretentious lyrics he'd committed to record. "Yes, star crossed in pleasure/The stream flows on by/Yes, as we are sated in leisure/We watch it fly". Whatever happened to slave ships and bells, books and candles?

Apart from the odd occasion when a few choice phrases seem uncannily right for their time ('Satisfaction' or 'Gimme Shelter', for example), the Stones have rarely been troubled into speaking 'great things' in their songs. As Jagger and Richards have long maintained, lyrics have always been given too much attention in rock criticism anyway: it's audiences who give songs their true meaning, and it's no secret that the organisation of sound, and the artists' positioning in the (sub)cultural scheme of things are profoundly more important.

Which is why 'Time Waits For No-One' is always described as "that sophisticated one, where Mick Taylor sounds like Carlos Santana": who remembers anything about its lyrics apart from the song title? The fact that Jagger sounded closer to Van Morrison than Mick Jagger was clearly more important, and appropriate too, reflecting an idiosyncratic outbreak of instrumental delicacy. At a time when bands were judged according to their technical prowess, 'Time Waits For No-One' meant that the Stones still had one foot (or at least a toe or two) in the 'rock school' camp.

LUXURY

According to Keith Richards, this song came to
him while he was driving from the Munich Hilton
to the studios, "fucked right out of my head and
the radio was playing this soul number, which I
still don't know the title of, but it had this chord
sequence". By the time it had travelled from ear
to brain, and then to tape, the reggae sounds
picked up in Jamaica in late 1972 had worked
their way to the foreground, providing a strong
opposing current to Richards' variation on
Bowie's 'Watch That Man' riff. Jagger had
perfected his poor-man patois, too.

When Bob Ludwig dug out the original
master-tape when remastering the Virgin CD, he
re-instated 30 seconds edited from the original.

DANCE LITTLE SISTER

During the mid-Sixties, bands could get away
with bar-room crowd-pleasers: by the mid-
Seventies, they invariably sounded dull, however much fun they were to record. The first
few seconds, where the guitar and drums
almost struggle to find the exact groove, are
precious, but from then on it was downhill all
the way. However, the return to no-nonsense

R&B appealed to Stu's perception of what he felt the Stones ought to be, so Nicky Hopkins sat this one out.

IF YOU REALLY WANT TO BE MY FRIEND

More convincing than 'Till The Next Goodbye', this soul ballad harked back to 'Let It Loose' from 'Exile', substituting that song's ragged splendour with the cultivated harmonies of vocal group Blue Magic. Had it been written a couple of years earlier, it probably would have been smothered in horns, but for the first time since late 1969, Jim Price and Bobby Keyes were not used.

SHORT AND CURLIES

When the police broke up the party at Keith's Redlands residence in 1967, someone decided to make light of the situation by playing Bob Dylan's 'Rainy Day Woman #12 & 35'. Dixon Of Dock Green pulling the place apart, and Bob singing 'Everybody must get stoned' – it must have been hysterical.

The comical country-like riff that drove Dylan's song along was revived on this similar-ly trivial one-liner, though "She's got you by the balls" was hardly a match for Bob's counter-cultural anthem.

FINGERPRINT FILE

Keith 'Superfly' Richards' wah-wah guitar, a cracking Wyman's bassline, and a filthy rhythm part from axeman Jagger conspired to make this one of the Stones' finest achievements of the decade.

Picking up from where 'Heartbreaker' left off, the song was six-and-a-half minutes of studio-enhanced paranoia, all dark corners, upturned collars and footsteps in the shadows, the album's only genuine lurch into the unknown. Jagger, with one eye still on an acting career, did himself plenty of favours, getting into character and rising to the occasion with an atmospheric vocal performance.

THE ROLLING STONES
BLACK AND BLUE

Black and Blue

(VIRGIN 7243-8-39499-2-2, RELEASED APRIL 1976)

"**R**ehearsing guitar players, that's what that one was about." Keith 'no bullshit' Richards' one-liners on the Stones back catalogue get straight to the heart of the matter, though on this occasion, he drastically undersells what's an unduly overlooked album.

Released to the fanfare of an extensive European tour, and previewed by what many consider to be a single that borders on the heretical, 'Black And Blue' found the Stones thrown into chaos by the departure of Mick Taylor (just as work on the record was about to begin). Had the trauma not arisen, one can only speculate what a son of 'It's Only Rock'n'Roll' might have sounded like: as it turned out, the disturbed intra-band politics invested the sessions with a creative tension that would otherwise have been absent.

Several guitarists were tried out during the making of the album, a situation which lent the proceedings an air of unreality. Jeff Beck one day, Peter Frampton the next, Wayne Perkins, Harvey Mandel, Rory Gallagher at other times, climaxing with the re-appearance of Ron Wood, confirming that the likeliest candidate all along was the man for the job. Taylor had

expressed frustration at the group's musical inertia, and besides, any songwriting ambitions he harboured were unlikely to get a look-in. Woody, as this profoundly good-natured man is affectionately known, already had a secondary solo career which gave him a creative free hand. Playing the Keith Richards' role in The Faces, his preference for rhythm/lead interplay suited the Stones – after all, that was how Richards and Jones started out.

Wood wasn't a *bona fide* member at any point during the sessions (he officially joined in February 1976, after Rod Stewart disbanded The Faces): indeed, both Harvey Mandel and Wayne Perkins made significant contributions to the album. Billy Preston, too, came into his own on 'Black And Blue', lending weight to the criticism that the Stones were increasingly at the mercy of their session players. It would be hard to imagine the Glimmer boys letting such a situation arise, but surrounded by such quality players, it's inevitable that some of their accomplices' ideas rubbed off. With one or two reservations, the results were definitely up a grade on the previous album. Shame the band went and spoiled it with their tasteless advertising campaign (in the States, at least), which depicted a woman bound by ropes with her legs apart. The slogan?: "I'm black and blue with the Rolling Stones and I love it." Hmm.

HOT STUFF

According to the detailed breakdown disseminated as part of the album packaging, 'Hot Stuff' was recorded on 30th March 1975 at Musicland, Munich, the studio used on all but one of the album tracks. And the intoxicating lead breaks, which weren't dissimilar to those favoured by The Isley Brothers a few years earlier, came courtesy of Harvey Mandel, one-time Canned Heat guitarist.

The song (though to be frank, it was more of a groove thing) hung on a bubbling Wyman bassline that continued on from where 'Fingerprint File' left off, with more 'Superfly' guitar-work from Richards. Plunging full-throttle

into the disco sounds then sweeping the American clubs, 'Hot Stuff' showed how the Stones could still dress themselves in contemporary influences and step out with conviction.

HAND OF FATE

Keith Richards later said that an American guitarist in a British band wouldn't have been right, but Wayne Perkins' contribution was every bit the equal of fellow countryman Mandel's, and far more in keeping with the band's sound. Jagger's tendency to bark, increasingly noticeable in concert, was beginning to find its way onto record, but on this occasion, it suited the song's mood well.

CHERRY OH BABY
(Eric Donaldson)

Unlike 'Luxury', which utilised reggae rhythms but balanced them with a riff plucked out of Keith's box of spares, this cover stayed faithful to Eric Donaldson's 1971 original. The novelty value soon became wearing, though, and 'Cherry Oh Baby' is one of the few songs in the band's catalogue that comes close to being unbearable. An inauspicious start for Ronnie Wood, reunited with his ex-Jeff Beck Group colleague, Nicky Hopkins. Next.

MEMORY MOTEL

Skirting the musical values championed by Radio 2, the Stones took on this big, sprawling ballad, tossed in a few "sha-la-laas" and survived. It was totally unlike anything the band had attempted before: Jagger, Richards and Billy Preston all seated at keyboards, Wayne Perkins on acoustic, Mandel electric and Keith no guitar at all. It would have been a wonderfully sentimental way to bow out, had it been the band's swan song – all on-the-road reminiscences of cities and the women who triggered them off. To cap it all, Jagger and Richards pulled off a remarkably touching vocal duet.

HEY NEGRITA

After working on 'Cherry Oh Baby' back in December 1974, Ronnie Wood returned towards the end of the sessions, and saved this hard-funk jam by out-Keithing Keith with some off-the-wall staccato guitar. The pair

broke ranks midway through with a cut-and-paste change in the rhythm, but even this failed to convince anyone that there was ever a song here in the first place. Good groove, though.

MELODY

There's a lot of Billy Preston on 'Black And Blue', nowhere more so than on 'Melody'. Again, another break with type, the band launched into a keyboard-dominated, lazy shuffle, offering Charlie Watts a rare (and no doubt most welcome) opportunity to reach for his brushes. Preston's piano leaves a trail of jazz phrases throughout the song, and his regular vocal interjections soon prompt Jagger into a call-and-response litany of screams and grunts. 'Melody' was the only track not taped at Musicland: it was recorded on The Rolling Stones' Mobile, in Rotterdam, in January 1975.

FOOL TO CRY

The band always had a silent sixth piano-playing member – first Ian Stewart, later Nicky Hopkins, and more recently Billy Preston. On 'Fool To Cry', Jagger played the keyboard part

himself (though he left the difficult bits, including the enigmatic string synth part, to Hopkins), indicating that it was probably his song.

The opening bars were every bit as shocking as anything the band had ever done, more Barry Manilow than Muddy or Berry. And its sentimental lyric bore none of the ass-slapping style that fans had been weaned on. Out of character, and even out of favour with some of the band (notoriously, Richards fell asleep during the song in Germany on the '76 tour), 'Fool To Cry' outschmaltzed all its competitors, with some wonderfully subtle dynamics and Richards delivering some of the most understated lead lines of his career.

CRAZY MAMA

'Black And Blue' closed in more familiar style, with Keith and Ronnie pointing the way forward to more strident interplay, and Jagger hot-tempered and raving. References to "cold blood murder" and "blown out brains" didn't have anything like the impact they might have done six years earlier, for by 1976, the Stones no longer epitomised either the hopes or the fears of any single subculture or generation.

Part Three
EMI & Beyond 1978-1994

Rolling Stones Records was never a truly independent record company. Instead, it was a trademark that could be hawked around from time to time, available to the highest bidder. EMI picked up the rights to the material in 1977 with a six-album deal. Then came CBS in 1983, who secure the rights to the next four. And now they're in the hands of Virgin (owned, of course, by EMI) who failed to mention Rolling Stones Records anywhere on 'Voodoo Lounge'.

Some Girls

(VIRGIN 7243-8-39505-2-2, RELEASED JUNE 1978)

A new permanent guitarist, a new six-album deal with EMI – and the shock of the new wave to contend with. But first, there was the problem of Keith Richards' 1977 Toronto drug bust. At one point, with the prospect of a lengthy prison spell hanging over him, it threatened to rip the band apart: instead it sealed his reputation as Wasted One No. 1, and helped to bridge the gap between the Stones as old farts and the blanked-out faces of the punk generation.

While no-one seriously believed that the band would convincingly reinvent themselves as punk rockers, 'Some Girls' was their grittiest set of songs since 'Exile', helping them through what were difficult times for long-in-the-tooth rock acts. With Richards preoccupied with beating the rap and, more critically, beating a decade-long drug habit, Jagger took the bait, took some guitar lessons from Ron Wood, and steered the band successfully into the next stage of their career.

Punk squeezed the last traces of R&B out of white guitar rock: blue notes were replaced by the furious white heat of endless on-beats, played so fast that there was little room for the syncopation on which the Stones had based their entire style. Nevertheless, the band proved remarkably adaptable. Claims that Jagger was more interested in costly cuisine and even more expensive girlfriends than he was in the band were roundly answered by the album.

Again produced by The Glimmer Twins, with engineer Chris Kimsey, work on 'Some Girls' began in October 1977 (over two years since their last studio sessions) at the Pathé-Marconi Studios, Paris. By the time they emerged, the following March, some forty-four songs had been recorded, remarkably fast work for a group who'd been seduced by the torpor that had set in during the early Seventies. Several album titles were considered, including 'More Fast Numbers' and 'Don't Heal My Girlfriend', before they settled on 'Some Girls'. Asked why that one, Keith replied, "because we couldn't remember their fucking names".

MISS YOU

Another in a short line of songs energised by a steamy American disco bassline, the choice of 'Miss You' as the single was a masterstroke. Eschewing the obvious route – 'going punk' – it found an alternative route into 1978, without the band inviting comparisons with their spottier, spikier contemporaries. Jagger's scat delivery was entirely in harmony with the breakdown of traditional musical values; Sugar Blue's masterful harmonica was not, but his sweet notes still sounded like fresh air; and the hook was as insistent as anything else going around that year.

An extended, Bob Clearmountain-remixed version, originally issued on 12", is currently unavailable on CD. Pity, because 'Miss You' sounds even better over eight-and-a-half minutes than it does over four.

WHEN THE WHIP COMES DOWN

Blame it on The Velvet Underground's 'Venus In Furs', but for the punk who liked all the trappings of the new nihilism, the whip was a vital S&M accessory. Jagger was obviously a close observer of the most vital subculture to hit the headlines since hippie days, and on 'Whip' he managed to drop in references to spitting, the dole, even an uncharacteristic reference to non-heterosexual sex. He also played a punkish guitar, and once again, shunned conventional singing in favour of the agitated, spoken-word effect. The times they must have been a-changin'.

A live version, recorded in June 1978 at the Midsouth Coliseum, Memphis, can be found on the 'Sucking In The Seventies' compilation.

JUST MY IMAGINATION
(Norman Whitfield/Barrett Strong)

Unlike the uninspired version of The Temptations' 'Ain't Too Proud To Beg' back in 1974, this was one of the band's more successful Motown covers. The sound was dense, with layers of guitars reducing Ian McLagan's Hammond organ to a mere murmur, yet stopped short of swamping the song's natural charm. In another age, the band might have issued this on single.

SOME GIRLS

What was the late-Seventies without the whiff of controversy? It wasn't quite sticking a safety pin through the queen's nose, but the more familiar charge of sexism, this time given a distinctly racial twist, by Jagger's declaration that "black girls just want to get fucked all night".

The Rev. Jesse Jackson led the campaign to get the song withdrawn, saying: "it is an insult to our race and degrading to our women". The Stones issued a statement expressing surprise that their "parody of certain stereotypical attitudes" was being taken seriously. The case for Jagger's depiction of women as appendages in a male-dominated world would have been far stronger, but he could hardly be described as a racist.

Today, of course, the lyric would barely raise a stir. Active female sexuality is now proudly acknowledged, and the Stones' notorious misogyny has been eclipsed by countless rap and metal bands. More than that, boys asserting their manliness in the symbolic pop arena just aren't taken that seriously any more.

LIES

Or 'When The Whip Comes Down' Mark Two. When The Sex Pistols sang 'Liar', it was aimed at the whole rotten world. In the Stones' hands, the adversary was far more specific: "Lies – whispered sweetly in my ear", "Lies – you dirty Jezebel". Guess some girls just can't be trusted, huh? Though it would never have made it onto the first Clash album, it was certainly in keeping with their second – not punk rock, but rockist punk.

FAR AWAY EYES

This, the band's first fully-fledged country excursion in several years, was so hideously incongruous, so excessively camp (Jagger performs like Dolly Parton addressing a Nashville convention) that it cut right through the contemporary critical divide. Add to that a witty lyric which told of blind faith, Bible Belt-style, and the union of form and content was complete. So complete, in fact, that many mistook the song to be a country pisstake which, as Keith Richards would be the first to admit, was not the band's intention. Perhaps that's why he thought Jagger had overdone his vocal part.

'Far Away Eyes' wasn't the only country song taped at the 'Some Girl' sessions. However, the far more excitable 'Claudine', inspired by the case of Claudine Longet – the ex-wife of Sixties crooner Andy Williams, who was convicted of shooting her lover – was shelved due to potential legal problems.

RESPECTABLE

Self-mockery is always an effective form of defence, and the Stones used that artistic device to cover themselves on this runaway slice of R&B, post-punk-style. Well, at least, for the opening verse, before the backhanded compliment gets switched to some First Lady or another. The song, which also appeared on single, is notable for Keith Richards' first Berry-inspired solo on a studio record since 1974.

BEFORE THEY MAKE ME RUN

Many cosmetic adjustments took place during the making of the album, with Jagger proving to be the chief engineer, barking out his instructions at rehearsals and studio jams. It all proved

worthwhile, because 'Some Girls' became the band's most critically-acclaimed record since 'Sticky Fingers'.

What 'Before They Make Me Run' added was something that a lifetime's free entry to Studio 51, Max's Kansas City or the Nashville couldn't buy – conviction. When Richards wrote this piece of confessional, laudably free from sentimentalism or regret, his trial was still months away. The badges screamed 'Keef Is Innocent', but even the man himself knew that some kind of judgement day awaited him – whether it be incarceration, a make-or-break clean-up, or perhaps both.

The song clearly marked the arrival of a new Richards, and in more than one way. In the past, he'd chosen not to stretch himself on the rare solo vocal outing: this time, even double-tracking the vocals couldn't hide the strain in his voice, and his delivery was genuinely unpredictable, full of pregnant pauses followed by flurries of garbled words. It's the way he's sung ever since.

BEAST OF BURDEN

It's not surprising that Stones ballads are usually the sole preserve of male singers, which makes 'Beast Of Burden' somewhat unique. Not only did Bette Midler cover the song, she also roped Jagger into making an appearance in the accompanying video.

The follow-up single to 'Miss You' in the States, 'Beast Of Burden' was good enough for Jagger to forget – for a moment – the sound of the suburbs beating all around him, and brave enough to risk a rare public demonstration of vulnerability: "Ain't I rough enough?/Ain't I tough enough?/Ain't I rich enough?/In love enough?/Oooo, ooh, please". Hear the crowds swoon on the live version, recorded on the winter 1981 US tour, which appeared on the flip of 'Going To A Go-Go' the following year. But not on CD.

SHATTERED

More streetwise rapping from Jagger over what's basically a one-riff exercise in repetition, propelled by a fine Ron Wood bassline, and with Mr. J himself on guitar. But exactly who, or what, is shattered? While the song reaches out towards the widely-perceived contemporary malaise ("Don't you know the crime rate is going up, up, up, up"), it can also be seen as a response to all the recent knocks, like the notorious Burchill/Parsons assault in *New Musical Express* which, with Dylan and the Stones foremost in mind, suggested we "take these gods and stuff them!". Alternatively, perhaps Jagger may just have been knackered.

'Everything Is Turning To Gold', an out-take from the Paris '77 sessions, first appeared on the flip of the American-only 'Shattered' 45, and has since been issued on the 'Sucking In The Seventies' CD.

Emotional Rescue
(VIRGIN 7243-8-39501-2-6, RELEASED JUNE 1980)

'**S**ome Girls', and its flagship 'Miss You', had kept the Stones afloat while many of their contemporaries (and those who followed them) offered no defence whatsoever. The big boys, like The Who and The Kinks, had become little more than American AOR fodder, while the progressive bands of the early Seventies were not having their contracts renewed. Old farts? Yes (Bill was already forty-plus); musically obsolete in the face of the rising anti-stars of the independent scene? Quite probably.

As the end of the decade approached, the world discovered that it didn't necessarily *need* the Stones any more, but 'Some Girls' suggested that it was still good to have them around. Not so 'Emotional Rescue', a facsimile of the previous album, but about 75% less convincing. Having been provoked into action by punk rock, testing the water and finding it surprisingly welcoming, the band quickly returned to that winning formula, not realising that musical expectations had changed, that coasting it was simply not enough any more. (It didn't last long: by the early Eighties, those lofty expectations had collapsed.)

'Emotional Rescue' remains one of the most forgettable moments in the band's thirty-year-plus history. Even the technical wonders which produced the thermographic photographs used on the cover were singularly unimpressive. Um, what else? The band returned to the Pathé-Marconi Studios in Paris, to record the bulk of it, with additional work being done at Compass Point Studio, Nassau, in the Bahamas. Its release was slightly delayed due to the problems surrounding the inclusion of 'Claudine'. Here's what you really ought to know: when Jagger embarked on the round of interviews to promote the album, he told one journalist: "There is no future in rock'n'roll". Listening to his latest album, it wasn't difficult to disagree with him.

DANCE
(Jagger/Richards/Wood)

Once the Stones find a groove, they tend to stick with it until the bitter end: this was the third consecutive studio album to kick off with a disco-funk number, and it was most definitely a case of third time unlucky.

It needn't have turned out quite so bad. "I saw 'Dance' as more of an instrumental, like Jr. Walker's 'Shotgun'," said Keith, "and Mick came up with reams of paper and lyrics. I thought it should be a minimal lyric, and Mick comes up with Don Giovanni!" Despite the presence of Max 'Wet Dream' Romeo on backing vocals, and ex-Santana man Michael Shrieve on percussion, what would have made a passable, one-minute scene-setting piece quickly outlasted its welcome. Those who regard being spanked or beaten up as a pleasant way of passing the time might like to know that the 'Sucking In The Seventies' compilation contains an alternative version, retitled 'If I Was A Dancer (Dance Part 2)'.

SUMMER ROMANCE

Originally taped in Paris in January 1978, as part of the 'Some Girls' sessions, this didn't make the grade first time round. Why this poor man's 'Respectable' was deemed good enough for 'Emotional Rescue' tells us much about the state of the band's creative health. "Nobody had any proper vision of it," admitted Jagger later, when recalling the making of the album.

SEND IT TO ME

Cod-reggae was a miserable genre at the best of times, but this lines up among its worst excesses. The "it" was, of course, a woman: Rumanian, Bulgarian, Albanian, Hungarian, blonde or brunette, rich or poor, even the girl next door, what did it matter? An increasing Left agenda in contemporary rock criticism only fuelled Jagger to ever more absurd lyrical depths. If this was the best the Stones could come up with, imagine what the 30 or so rejected tracks must have sounded like?

LET ME GO

Further evidence that the templates laid down on 'When The Whip Comes Down' and 'Respectable' were already wearing thin. Wood and Richards' interplay was effective enough, but there was nothing to suggest that the song was little more than filler.

INDIAN GIRL

The measured tempo of the country-tinged 'Indian Girl' brought the best out of Jagger's voice, saw the reintroduction of the steel guitar, and the return of an old accomplice, Jack Nitzsche, who arranged the horns. The song sent a confused, pre-Live Aid message concerning the Equatorial continents, gave Jagger an opportunity for some *vox Latino*, and gave those who'd bought the record blindly a small something to cheer about.

WHERE THE BOYS GO

When the band first tried this out, during the 'Some Girls' sessions, they wisely discarded it. A brave Keith Richards solo briefly alleviates the monotony of this sub-Members piece of drivel, complete with some exaggerated (to the point of pain) 'Cockney punk' vocals from Jagger. Unfortunately, he forgot that priceless piece of advice from Fats Domino, so there was no escape from the 'lads out on a Saturday night' lyric: posing, fighting, football, dancing and, of course, finding a "piece of arse", the latter a strangely Anglicised enunciation from the man who virtually invented Mid-Atlanticism.

DOWN IN THE HOLE

Encircled by the hollow ring of going-nowhere-fast peppy power-pop was a blessing for the moodiest burst of blues performed by the band since they walked off stage at the El Mocambo club in Toronto in 1977. A grainy harmonica, courtesy of Sugar Blue, a Jagger lyric which managed not to stray too far from the theme, and a ringing bassline that threatened to steal the show from the guitars, all contributed towards a rare album highlight.

EMOTIONAL RESCUE

Probably the band's weakest-ever 45, 'Emotional Rescue' sought to revive memories of 'Miss You' but failed dismally. Jagger's falsetto was a poor substitute for the Gibb brothers' soaring harmonies, which had dominated late-Seventies pop; and, besides, the dull thud of the rhythm was third-rate. Disco music, at its best, took pleasure-seeking to new heights: 'Emotional Rescue' was the cue for getting the last bus home.

Written by Jagger on electric piano, and first recorded with Ron Wood on bass and Charlie Watts, the song was also prepared in 'dub version' form – almost always a recipe for disaster in the hands of white rock/pop bands. Thankfully, that was kept in the vaults.

SHE'S SO COLD

"I'm so hot for her/And she's so cold." Where was Jimmy Miller when we needed him? Where was Keith Richards (probably doing cold turkey, hence Jagger's dominant role for the second album in succession)? Repetition in the hands of bands like Can or The Velvet Underground could be beautiful: but it didn't suit the Stones one bit.

ALL ABOUT YOU

Latterly, the press like to distinguish between Jagger's organising brain and Richards' heart of Stone. Insiders close to the band tend to disagree, but when the blue saxes which introduce this song melt away, leaving the naked flame of Richards' voice to burn alone, it's not difficult to see why such a clear demarcation exists in the popular imagination.

Richards rarely writes full lyrics, preferring to tinker with what Jagger comes up with, but on 'All About You', something clearly troubled him. Prior to recording the album, he'd split with his long-time girlfriend Anita Pallenberg, and it's probably no coincidence that 'All About You' concerns the end of a relationship. The words are bitter and twisted, as they often are in the aftermath of emotional breakdown, but the music – and Richards' performance in particular – is precious, philosophical and conciliatory, as is the pay-off line: "So how come I'm still in love with you?".

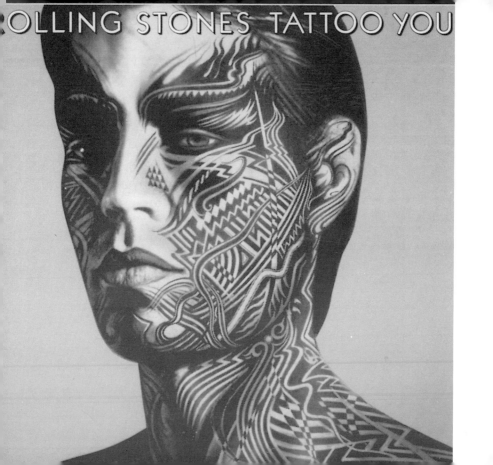

Tattoo You

(VIRGIN 7243-8-39502-2-5, RELEASED AUGUST 1981)

Having worn their best 'been-there, done-that, can-still-do-it' faces for 'Some Girls', the pancake had clearly cracked by the time of 'Emotional Rescue'. The band weren't unduly worried, though, having topped both the US and UK album charts. With no particular creative place to go, and yet another contract-filling album on the schedule, they began work on 'Tattoo You' by ordering up listening copies of out-takes from the archive, some dating back to 'Goats Head Soup'. It wasn't the finest of omens.

The mock-tattooed faces of Jagger and Richards which adorned the sleeve served to hide the ageing process (the rehabilitation of old wave stars wasn't fully complete until Live Aid in 1984/5), and, like the 'It's Only Rock'n'Roll' graffiti campaign, hitched a ride on an increasingly popular subcultural fad. But they couldn't hope to hide the sound of straws being clutched, a sound which was to characterise their career for much of the decade. Oddly, they made one or two lucky dips this time round, enough at least to ensure that 'Tattoo You', unfocused and third rate as it was by the band's standards, was a marginally less bitter pill than the previous set.

Personal relationships within the band weren't all they could be: Richards was still adjusting to life without smack, while Jagger was still searching for a niche in a post-punk world. Most exposed of all, perhaps, was the notable lack of spark from the guitar players. The Richards/Wood dream ticket looked good in the publicity stills, and Wood's presence certainly introduced a much-needed 'feel good' factor into the band's activities, after a distinctly standoffish period during the mid-Seventies. Yet, those cynics who felt that Ron's style would be cramped playing second fiddle to Richards started to sound like sages. 'Start Me Up', the first single to be culled from the album, was, after all, no 'Honky Tonk Women'.

START ME UP

It was, as one writer put it, like punk never happened. As the Seventies closed, a chart takeover by radical ex-punk acts like PiL, Joy Division and Siouxsie and The Banshees looked clearly on the cards. The children of The Velvet Underground, Marc Bolan and Captain Beefheart were set to claim the Eighties as their own. Instead, the new cultural politics of rampant individualism seemed to undermine the short-lived independent quest for new musical spaces. 'Classic' values – unremitting celebration of the star, musical simplicity, and above all an unashamed populism – had returned.

For many years, the Stones announced each new album with a ballad, or a disco-inspired number – anything, in fact, but a typically Stones-like rocker. 'Start Me Up', all blocked chords and clipped vocals, was the Stones by rote – a musical equivalent of the fad for reproduction antique furniture that flourished throughout the decade. In truth, no-one particularly minded the band's decision to sod contemporary fashion: that, after all, was how they delivered an album like 'Exile'. It was simply that 'Start Me Up' was too studied, too counterfeit Stones.

The song didn't start out that way. It began as a reggae tune as far back as the 'Black And Blue' sessions, was presented with a rock backbeat during the making of 'Some Girls', before being given the 'Brown Sugar' makeover for this album. On the face of it, it worked, and the band were rewarded with their biggest international hit of the decade. They responded by opening their 1989 'Steel Wheels' tour with the song.

HANG FIRE

Originally taped in Paris in January 1978 as the PC-unfriendly 'Lazy Bitch', 'Hang Fire' was a fast, throwaway 'Some Girls' out-take which eventually became a single in the US. Back home, the lyrics – a glib reading of unemployment and avarice – might not have won them too many friends ("In the sweet old country where I come from/Nobody ever works/Nothing ever gets done"). Power pop with a spineless chorus didn't make for that memorable Stones moment.

SLAVE

One of many jams recorded during the 'Black And Blue' sessions, 'Slave' originally featured Sonny Rollins on sax, Billy Preston on organ, Nicky Hopkins on piano and Jeff Beck on guitar, though the latter's part was erased for this final version. The lyric consisted of little more than an occasional 'Don't wanna be your slave" (apparently assisted by Pete Townshend), and the backing was similarly rudimentary. Like The Beatles, the Stones were certainly no Can or Cream when it came to jamming.

The version on the recent Virgin CD edition of 'Tattoo You' boasts an additional 90 seconds of material, though it was hardly the most inspiring of gifts.

LITTLE T&A

'Little T&A' gave Richards the chance to proclaim, with some pride, that "the heat's raiding tracks are fading", that while his scars were healing, the dealers were "squealing". That was the good news. The Stones weren't chided for being 'old farts' purely because of their age. It was the atti-

TATTOO YOU : EMI & BEYOND 1978-1994

tudes they carried with them which were at least as damning – their odd line in 'authenticity' (they were the real thing, punks weren't, for example), their thoroughly compromised view of the establishment and their rampant sexism. 'Little T&A', an 'Emotional Rescue' out-take (not too encouraging, that), was little more than you'd expect a bunch of seasoned roadies to come up with. People were beginning to learn how to treat the Stones with the kind of disrespect they reserved for others.

BLACK LIMOUSINE
(Jagger/Richards/Wood)
Once again, all the basic parts were there – rockaboogie rhythm, nice guitar break, Stu's Johnnie Johnson impressions buried deep in the mix. Better played, and certainly better recorded than their 1964 Chicago recordings, this nostalgic R&B number (more than loosely based on Jimmy Reed's 'You Don't Have To Go') had a survivalist tone ("now look at your face baby... and look at me") which could have referred to Andrew Oldham or any number of blasts from the past.

NEIGHBOURS
Something of a rarity in that it was recorded specifically for this album, 'Neighbours' actually suggested that by delving into the archive for the bulk of their 'new' material, the Stones were doing themselves a favour. Charlie Watts' kit was desensitised by the onset of the 'booming' Eighties drum sound (a false economy, though, like the new political ideology it provided the soundtrack to), and 'Neighbours' was ultimately reduced to a loud-sounding nothing.

WORRIED ABOUT YOU
Jagger's falsetto, and a guitar break which sounded suspiciously similar to Wayne Perkins' efforts on 'Hand Of Fate' clearly confirmed the origin of this second out-take from 'Black And Blue'.

TOPS
A cast-off from 'Goats Head Soup', recorded in Jamaica late in 1972, this was the oldest song on the album. 'Tops' was given a more contemporary production sheen, particularly

noticeable on the drums, Mick Taylor's lead guitar lines were retained (which explains why he was miffed at not receiving a credit on the album), and while the song was hardly a classic, it at least moved with less of the wooden predictability that had become the norm. One of those soulful kinds of ballads, it might have been fun in the hands of Janis Joplin.

HEAVEN

Hey, perhaps marrying Sylvester and Santana wasn't a bad idea at all. 'Heaven' wasn't in-yer-face disco, nor was it overly precious. After almost a second album's worth of hearing the Stones sleepwalking, 'Heaven' – less a song, more a mood piece with one or two pleasant chord changes – begs for attention. One of the few tracks specially taped for the album, it was unexpected and surprisingly effective.

NO USE IN CRYING
(Jagger/Richards/Wood)

Originally recorded for 'Emotional Rescue', 'No Use In Crying' was worth committing to tape purely for the Mick'n'Keith-'round-the-mike-stand factor. Though mildly evocative of 'Time Is On My Side', the song was too clinically produced to ever fully capture the camaraderie, circa '64-style.

WAITING ON A FRIEND

The early Eighties wasn't notable for too many ground-shaking events in the rock world, but the ubiquity of the video promo was the nearest thing to revolutionary change. Often, the accompanying images proved to be more memorable than the song they were supposed to sell, but on 'Waiting On A Friend', director Michael Lindsay-Hogg (who'd shot *Rock And Roll Circus* back in 1968) got it just about right. The song's lazy, amicable mood, accompanied by the sight of Mick and Keith meeting on a New York street, seemed almost touching – a word you'd hardly equate with the Stones' latter-day work. Oh, but there was acrimony ahead...

Undercover

(CBS CDCBS 450200-2, RELEASED NOVEMBER 1983)

Despite the success of the previous trilogy of albums, it was difficult to imagine the Stones wielding anything like the influence they once had. Throughout the Seventies, they'd bathed in the afterglow of the 'Greatest Rock'n'Roll Band In The World' legend that provided a welcoming shadow to hide behind whenever the going got rough. That's why CBS forked out a massive six million pounds per album deal for their next four records in August 1983, just prior to the release of this last new set for EMI. The Stones were the jewel in any roster of artists, but as the decade progressed, it became clear that this was because of the goodwill attached to their name, rather than any profits they might generate. Dozens of younger acts now outsold them by very large margins.

By the early Eighties, it was difficult to perceive the Stones' work in any way other than grand spectacle and consumer fetishism. Once, they'd provided the theme tunes which gave their audiences the ammunition with which to empower their own lives. Now, their records were merely incidental music in a world which no longer counted mass popular music as its prime force for change.

That the Stones understood this is evident by the difficulties they experienced in finding a niche other than that of living legends persevering in the face of increasing obsolescence. In an increasingly competitive climate, it was merely enough for them to appear as survivors. Their 1981/82 world tour was greeted with mass approval, but like an old Hollywood movie, the crowds shuffled out of the stadium doors having witnessed the timeless resolution that a happy ending always brings. If there were tears, it was merely because 'this may be the last time', not that the Stones were exposed merely as entertainers, rather than as agitators for something that was never their own making in the first place.

UNDERCOVER OF THE NIGHT

The 'oxygen of publicity' was one of the decade's most potent catchphrases, and the free press which Andrew Oldham generated twenty years earlier now had to be paid for. By shooting a video which featured as its climax the sight of Jagger being shot through the head by central American gangsters (remember, this was the man who, years earlier, had thwarted the publication of a book entitled 'The Man Who Shot Mick Jagger'), the Stones spent their money wisely – 'Undercover Of The Night' got extensive publicity after the video was censored on the grounds of taste.

The song's hard funk rhythm was partially obscured by the band's headlong surge into modern production techniques, with extensive use of sampling, phasing, in fact the whole repertoire of mixing-desk trickery. Coming shortly after the Empire had struck back in the Falklands, this tale of Central and South American governmental corruption was somewhat ambivalent. Nevertheless, by conflating political violence and the white heat of technological rock, the Stones managed to hit a contemporary nerve.

The dub version, another sop to fashion, which appeared on the 12", is currently unavailable on CD.

SHE WAS HOT

Chuck Leavell provided the keyboards on 'Undercover Of The Night'; this second single, conceived in more traditional rockaboogie fashion, tempted tinkling Stu back onto the stool.

Strange that Jagger's hollering verses conjured up memories of his sterling work on 'Exile', for in this context, the effect was distinctly underwhelming. The accompanying promo video, which featured dancer Anita Morris provoking all manner of virile posturing (climaxing with the band's trouser-flies bursting with over-excitement) was a bad idea made excruciating.

'I Think I'm Going Mad', a slow country-wise side-dish from the 'Emotional Rescue' sessions, was unearthed for the B-side of the 'She Was Hot' single.

TIE YOU UP
(THE PAIN OF LOVE)

Anyone wanna buy an old 'Black And Blue' advertising poster? Funk'n'raunch was the defining feature of 'Undercover' and 'Tie You Up' is probably the album's most representative example of that simple aim.

WANNA HOLD YOU

It was encouraging that Jagger and Richards began work on the album by spending some time together working on new material. 'Wanna Hold You' was one of the products of this attempt to break the hideous cycle of starting a new record by sifting through the offcuts of the previous sessions.

The song found Richards taking his sole vocal bow on the album and, unlike much of his post-Toronto work, he was in upbeat mood, very much the man in the grip of a new love affair (he married model Patti Hansen a month after the album's release).

FEEL ON BABY

Reggae might have peaked during the late Seventies, but that didn't prevent the Stones having another go, with top session players Robbie Shakespeare and Sly Dunbar playing it like it is. An instrumental mix of the song appeared on the flip of the 'Undercover Of The Night' 12".

TOO MUCH BLOOD

The use of the studio as an auxiliary instrument was tested to its limits on the 12"-only, Arthur Baker-mixed 'Dance' and 'Dub' versions of this song which neatly encapsulated the growing fascination for another Eighties phenomenon, the serial killer. The Sugarhill brass section provided the horns, while Keith and Ronnie played out their guitarists/'mad axemen' roles in the promo video by wielding electrical saws.

PRETTY BEAT UP
(Jagger/Richards/Wood)

The slick disco horn-playing of David Sanborn squirmed over a roughed-up disco backing, which was Ronnie Wood's greatest contribution to the album. But as with much of the set, the high-profile drum-sound still overshadowed the sound that makes the Stones matter – the guitars. That's no bad reflection on Charlie Watts, more a complaint that they were seemingly content to slip into the ubiquitous beat of '83 for no other reason than the fact that they couldn't be bothered to say no.

TOO TOUGH

The anachronistic sound of the riff, plus the slightly elevated tone of the chorus probably confirms the rumour that this began life as an instrumental titled 'Cellophane Trousers' back in 1975. The riff can be dated back further, as it bears a strong resemblance to 'I'm Going Down', a reject from the first Mick Taylor sessions in 1969, which later found its way onto the 'Metamorphosis' collection. Given the grittier production the song cried out for, it could have been memorable rather than marginal.

ALL THE WAY DOWN

This is the kind of ineffectual mid-paced rocker that those who passed up on the Stones' Eighties work imagined must have cluttered up all their later albums.

IT MUST BE HELL

They could have done worse than see out the record on the ghost of the riff from 'Soul Survivor', but much of what made that 'Exile' track truly climactic was missing here. A watchful CBS must have been glad they'd also picked up the rights to the band's post-1971 back catalogue.

Dirty Work

(CBS CDCBS 86321, RELEASED MARCH 1986)

The band went their separate ways after 'Undercover'. Nothing unusual in that: since the early Seventies, they'd go for weeks, sometimes months on end without seeing one another. Jagger always had a hectic social calendar to attend to; Richards inevitably retreated into a dimly-lit existence; Wood sometimes joined him, or else turned up jamming in some strange corner of the world; Wyman busied himself with production work, the occasional solo project and an increasingly headline-grabbing personal life; and Watts was simply relieved to be back home with his family.

Progressively, the lay-off periods got longer, and almost two years passed before they reconvened for 'Dirty Work'. More significantly, twenty years after the first rumours that he might launch his own solo career, Jagger had defied all the advice (from a Dr. Richards in particular) and split The Glimmer Twins right down the middle by releasing a solo album. Basically a Stones album with the rock'n'roll diluted, and the dance beats accented, 'She's The Boss' wouldn't have infuriated the rest of the band quite as much had its release – in March 1985 – not come smack in the middle of the sessions for the forthcoming Stones LP.

Live Aid raised money for a good cause, though its most enduring achievement was probably in wiping away any last traces of punk's iconoclasm, further validating the Stones' continuing adventures. It also revealed a deepening of the split. After the band had decided not to play, Jagger hastily arranged a solo appearance, his first. (Richards and Wood's attempt to upstage him by sidling up to Bob Dylan at the end of the US leg of the show backfired when Bob played an alternative set to the one they'd rehearsed.)

The sparks flew more publicly in the weeks prior to the release of 'Dirty Work'. Rumours flew around suggesting that things had got so bad that Jagger and Richards would never be able to work again; and that Don Covay and Bobby Womack were being considered as Mick's potential replacements. It all made the most readable copy on the band since the Toronto days, and there'd be plenty more of that just around the corner.

ONE HIT (TO THE BODY)
(Jagger/Richards/Wood)

Despite the change in co-producer (long-time partner Chris Kimsey sat this one out in favour of Steve Lillywhite), the battle between top-heavy drums and grungy rhythm guitars continued to be unsatisfactorily resolved on 'Dirty Work'. Producers, ever-mindful of rock's new conservatism, couldn't resist foregrounding the toe-tapping elements.

It didn't quite spoil 'One Hit', though the song never quite lived up to the clash of acoustic/electric guitars in the opening few bars. Lillywhite's fondness for a bright, clear sound (he'd previously worked with dull-but-huge stadium-rockers U2) brought the acoustic high into the mix, slightly buried the uncredited Jimmy Page on lead, and brought his wife Kirsty

MacColl along to assist on backing vocals.

A 'London Mix' was also effected for the 12", but like most remixes, detracts from rather than adds anything to the song. More essential was a glimpse at the promotional video, where director Russell Mulcahy made the most of the Jagger/Richards feud by concocting a virtual sparring match between the pair.

FIGHT
(Jagger/Richards/Wood)

Fast and furious, tense and brimming with latent aggression, 'Fight' was born of Richards' frustration at the end of another dismal recording session. Jagger, tail up and eager to stamp his authority, was in no mood for prissiness – and his performance transforms 'Fight' into a perfect anthem for the steroid-drenched-lager-lout-next-door.

HARLEM SHUFFLE
(Relf/Nelson)

The first single from the album, and the first non-Jagger/Richards 45 since 'It's All Over Now' back in 1964 (excepting the live 'Going

To A Go-Go'), 'Harlem Shuffle' had long been a favourite of Keith's.

Something of Bob and Earl's sassy original was retained (and the presence of Bobby Womack and Don Covay on backing vocals was a boon), though Chuck Leavell's keyboard approximation of the horn riff wasn't wholly endearing. Two extended versions of dubious quality appeared on the 12". These, the 'NY Mix' and 'London Mix' have yet to appear on CD.

HOLD BACK

Or don't hold back. Jagger didn't. That's why he proffered this piece of advice, "the voice of experience, a word from the wise". Four songs into the album, and the grizzled voice which had revealed itself in concert during the 1978 and 1981-82 tours had now become the norm in the studio. The voice of experience, or of exhaustion?

TOO RUDE
(Roberts)

At one stage, 'Too Rude' was considered as a potential album title, but this low-key reggae cover, featuring Keith and veteran Jamaican star Jimmy Cliff on vocals, was hardly the perfect title track, despite some heavy dub echo effects courtesy of Lillywhite.

WINNING UGLY

Once again, some fine guitar sparring was undercut by a top-heavy drum track and a dodgy keyboard. The story might have been different had the song been written and recorded in a different era. Once again, 'New York' and 'London' mixes of the song were made for 12" purposes.

BACK TO ZERO
(Jagger/Richards/Leavell)

"I'm looking to the future, I keep glancing back." However much Jagger tried to lay false, sometimes contradictory trails, his lyrics always had some kind of tale to tell, even if it was couching his own career misgivings against the background of potential world destruction. He could have chosen a better song than Bowie's 'Fashion' on which to base the verses, though.

DIRTY WORK
(Jagger/Richards/Wood)

Sgt. Major Jagger's barking mad vocals lend an unwelcome flatness to 'Dirty Work', but even that failed to suppress the finest 30 seconds or so on the record when, on the break, the twin guitars meshed together, creating a fleeting moment of transcendence. Chuck Leavell was probably under-used on the song, but that was a minor oversight compared with the drum-heavy mix.

HAD IT WITH YOU
(Jagger/Richards/Wood)

Jagger singing a rare piece of Keith Richards' vitriol aimed squarely at his good self? It's an unlikely scenario, but clearly quite true: such was the extent that Jagger could detach himself from a song's meaning. He turned in a fine harmonica break, too, while the sax came

courtesy of all-rounder Woody.

After lines like: "It is such a sad thing to watch a good love die/I've had it up to here, babe/I've got to say goodbye...", few predicted much of a future for the band.

SLEEP TONIGHT

This Richards-sung ballad bore little trace of Jagger, but a probable piano contribution from Keith's buddy Tom Waits. It also sounded like a swansong, littered with words lifted from twenty-plus years of the Jagger/Richards back catalogue: "sympathy", "shadows", "memory", "cold", "moon". It could have been coincidence, but the mood was obviously reflective, and even came with its own adios: "I wish you baby, all the best". (He was less charitable on 'You Don't Move Me', on his 1988 solo LP, 'Talk Is Cheap'.)

Richards wasn't to know when he recorded 'Sleep Tonight' that one of the Stones – the Sixth – wouldn't be coming back. For on December 12 1985, Ian Stewart died of a massive heart attack. Never again would the band hear his immortal, "Come on my little shower of shit, you're on". He was, according to Keith, "The glue that held the bits together", and a little bit of that glue – his inimitable boogie-woogie piano chords – was isolated to provide a touching, uncredited eleventh track on the album.

Steel Wheels

(CBS 465752-2, RELEASED SEPTEMBER 1989)

There was something immediately uplifting about 'Steel Wheels', though it certainly wasn't its nondescript cover (which at least spared us from the spectacle of the unflattering figures in primary colours on the cover of 'Dirty Work'). It might have had something to do with the news that Jagger and Richards had spent some time together in Barbados, patching up their differences. Or the fact that the group had worked up enough passion about their craft – and, one imagines, their own history – to return to Morocco to record parts for one song. (Of course, they could have achieved the desired effect by sampling, which only confirms that they'd rediscovered a hint of romance about their work.)

There was little doubt that 'Steel Wheels' was the best Stones album for at least a decade. They'd regained some of the appetite they'd lost after the 'Some Girls' sessions; 'playing the studio' was relegated to second, in favour of coming up with better material and a tolerable sound. When all seemed lost, the Stones surprised everyone, maybe even themselves, by playing as if they still had something to prove.

A lot had happened since 'Dirty Work' prompted so much dirty laundry to fly into the public's face. Charlie had taken his big band on tour and released an album of jazz standards. Keith had been Musical Director on a concert film/biography of his mentor Chuck Berry, and produced and played on Aretha Franklin's version of 'Jumpin' Jack Flash'. He'd also released his first solo record, 'Talk Is Cheap' (which got better reviews than Jagger's but sold far fewer copies) and toured with his X-Pensive Winos band. Ronnie Wood was fast-gaining respect as one of the few rock artists who could really paint. And he toured with Bo Diddley.

Meanwhile, main malcontent Mick released a second solo set, 'Primitive Cool' and toured Australia – playing a good proportion of songs from the Stones' catalogue. And then there was Bill Wyman's affair and subsequent marriage to teenager Mandy Smith, which overnight made him the second most famous Stone. Despite having fathered several teenagers between them, the band could still raise the odd whiff of scandal.

Mick and Keith's reconciliation in Barbados in January 1989 went well, and the pair emerged with the basis of several songs. Charlie Watts joined them in February, with Bill and Ron following early in March for rehearsals in Eddie Grant's Blue Wave Studios. The album was recorded at Air Studios in Montserrat during five weeks in March and April, with Chris Kimsey reinstated as co-producer.

SAD SAD SAD

It didn't quite have the debauchery of 'Rocks Off', or the leisured cool of 'Honky Tonk Women' or 'Tumbling Dice', but there was no doubting that 'Sad Sad Sad' was a more convincing revival of the band's rock'n'roll fortunes than anything they'd come up with in the previous decade. Richards was back to his thrilling old self and as audible as he should be; Wood's bassline buzzed with an unStones-like abandon; the Kick Horns brass section were

far more suited to the band than the fashionable experiments in that department during the previous years; and Jagger was... Jagger – sounding only as good as the band behind him: thankfully, they were cooking.

MIXED EMOTIONS

Towards the end of Andrew Solt's *25 x 5* video history of the band, there is some studio footage of Jagger and Richards working on this track. Eyeballing each other, their fingers fumbling for the right chords, their voices struggling to find the notes, it reconnected an element of human drama to their music. It gave 'Mixed Emotions' that extra dimension always missing on 'Start Me Up', and Jagger's let's-make-it-up response to Keith's 'You Don't Move Me' ("Let's bury the hatchet," etc.) was made all the more effective by the passionate chorus, which was light years away from their hamfisted jabs of late.

Chris Kimsey's remix, which first appeared on the 12" vinyl edition, can now be found on the Japanese-only 'Another Side Of Steel Wheels' CD (CBS CSCS 5116). The single featured the non-album 'Fancyman

Blues', originally taped for George Martin's 'After The Hurricane', a fundraising project for the victims of Hurricane Hugo, which decimated Montserrat late in 1989.

TERRIFYING

The Watts/Wyman engine-room, stoked up on funk fuel, gave Jagger an opportunity to drop his tendency to bark aggressively whenever a microphone was thrust under his nose. He did, and instead turned in one of those accentuated mood-mumbling vocals which found favour in the mid-Seventies, on material like 'Fingerprint File' and 'Hot Stuff'.

HOLD ON TO YOUR HAT

Like 'Sad Sad Sad', 'Hold On To Your Hat' was a no-holds-barred Stones rocker, with Ron Wood again on bass and Jagger duetting with Richards on guitar. With Bill away attending to the business of his forthcoming marriage, the four-piece – pushed to the limits by a newly-energised Charlie Watts – came as close as they'd ever come to replicating punk rock.

HEARTS FOR SALE

The forced anguish in Jagger's voice didn't do this middling rocker much good, though his finely-controlled harmonica break did. Ultimately, 'Hearts For Sale' was filler.

BLINDED BY LOVE

The melody shared a nodding acquaintance with their rejected 1965 ballad, 'Blue Turns To Grey'; the acoustic feel was given an added country flavour by Phil Beer's fiddle-playing; and the lyrics drew sustenance from 'betrayals' throughout the ages. Samson, Mark Anthony, the abdicating King Edward, 1all 'crumbled' after being 'blinded by love' warns Mick. Thanks, mate.

ROCK AND A HARD PLACE

Airwave-friendly enough to become the second single from the album, 'Rock And A Hard Place' really belonged back in a mid-Eighties wine bar. Its clean sound, peppered with era-defining blasts of grating brass notes, bubbly bass and call-and-response backing vocals, tended to blunt the general impression

the collector's CD (466 918-2) given free with 'Collection 1971-1989', a 12-CD set issued by CBS but now – with the exception of the bonus disc, which also contained 'Cook Cook Blues', the non-album flip of 'Rock And A Hard Place' – rendered obsolete by Virgin's recent activities. Far more convenient is the afore-mentioned Japanese 'Another Side Of Steel Wheels' CD, which contains all four remixes.

CAN'T BE SEEN

Jagger's absence from the heart of 'Dirty Work' soured the sessions, but – despite those who prefer to see the band as Richards' vehicle – it was his committed return to the fold which helped put 'Steel Wheels' on course. His absence on Keith's 'Can't Be Seen' suggests that the song may have once been destined for 'Talk Is Cheap'.

ALMOST HEAR YOU SIGH
(Jagger/Richards/Jordan)

This, co-written by Keith with his chief col-laborator on 'Talk Is Cheap', drummer Steve Jordan, definitely dates from his solo

that the band had thoroughly purged itself of pandering to US-provoked AOR values.

The song – originally titled 'Steel Wheels' – was edited for 7" purposes, and extended for a 'Dance Mix', 'Oh-Oh Hard Dub Mix', 'Bonus Beats Mix' (available on the CD single) and a 'Michael Bauer Mix' (which turned up on sessions. Jagger redrafted the lyrics, with a little help from brother Chris (credited, as on 'Blinded By Love', as 'Literary Editor'), Richards displayed some rudimentary classical guitar skills, and a trio of backing vocalists "ooh-oohed" – more in the style of Vaughan Williams than 'Sympathy For The Devil'.

When issued on single, 'Almost Hear You Sigh' was backed by the non-LP Jagger/Richards original, 'Wish I'd Never Met You'.

CONTINENTAL DRIFT

With the album almost complete, the final act was to visit Tangier, Morocco – the band's spiritual home during 1967 and Brian Jones' ever since (he's now an icon among the locals, who remember the keen interest he took in their music during several visits).

Jagger and keyboard player Matt Clifford had already laid the foundations for 'Continental Drift' back at Air Studios. Although the basis of the song stuck strictly to the familiar 4/4 rhythm, the lengthy instrumental break used a spiralling, trance-like

effect which lent itself perfectly to the shrill, hypnotic sounds of the Master Musicians Of Jajouka, led by Bachir Attar, who remembers meeting Jones as a child.

BREAK THE SPELL

Ardent Stones-watchers would have noticed yet another nostalgic touch here: the sparse, controlled 'Break The Spell' sounded very much like an updated 'Looking Tired', left unreleased since the mid-Sixties.

SLIPPING AWAY

Keith's 'Slipping Away' confirmed that, by the end of the Eighties, his soulful ballads were at least as welcome as yet another riff-rocker. What his voice lacked in dexterity and aggression was more than compensated by its gravelly warmth, which belied his steely public image. For the second album in succession, Richards was entrusted with saying goodbye: like waving off a kindly grandmother at the end of a holiday, his songs encapsulated that lump-in-the-throat "is this really the last time?" dread.

OLLING STONES VOODOO LOUNGE

Voodoo Lounge

(CDV 2750, RELEASED JULY 1994)

Two important things happened between the ending of the 'Steel Wheels' tour and the release of this, the band's twentieth studio album, thirty years after their first. It sealed a new £25 million deal with Virgin Records, inked back in November 1991. And it was the first without Bill Wyman, who finally called it a day in January 1993.

Of course, plenty more solo projects had come and gone during this, the lengthiest hiatus of all. It didn't seem to matter, though, for the entire 'Steel Wheels' experience – album, world tour and two videos – had been meticulously planned and executed, and more to the point, had engendered a new basis from which to proceed on band matters. Time for non-Stones activities after the tour was part of the long-term plan, and as part of this new world-view, solo activities didn't have to threaten the band's existence any more.

Desperation and ill feeling had been purged from the camp. What couldn't be predicted was the musical sea change which took place between the final months of the decade and 1993, when they began working on 'Voodoo Lounge'. Grunge, a hybrid of punk and metal which cut across the traditions of both vanguard experimentalism and classic songwriting, played into the hands of guitar-based acts with a rich past.

Neil Young stopped making the idiosyncratic lapses into computer-driven drivel or rock'n'roll pastiche by concentrating on what he did best. Led Zeppelin and Jimi Hendrix, still viewed with suspicion in the late-Eighties, shared a posthumous renaissance. Singer-songwriters, blues players, even country music became eminently marketable again. And supposedly unreformable Gods-of-old like Eric Clapton and Rod Stewart, thanks largely to MTV's 'Unplugged' series, began to sound like stars again.

The onus was on the big names to show their best hands and, liberated by the need to try on the latest suit and strap on the latest gizmo, they all seemed to seize the moment. The Stones, always acutely aware of any dramatic shifts of taste (sometimes to their detriment), responded as well as anyone could have expected them to. Armed with some of their best material since the early Seventies, and with a sympathetic co-producer in Don Was, they emerged in mid-1994 with 'Voodoo Lounge' – the kind of album no-one thought they were ever capable of making again. Like 'Steel Wheels', they couldn't sustain the heat for the whole duration, but 'Voodoo Lounge' even made that return to form sound half-hearted.

LOVE IS STRONG

Ever since 1971's 'Brown Sugar', the Stones have unveiled a new album with a single, which usually sets the tone for what was to follow. 'Love Is Strong' opened with a short drum burst, the guitars scrambled to find their way into the beat and Jagger blew a mean harp – all before the song settled.

For the first time in years, Watts sounded like he was in the same room as the band, and Jagger's voice – put through the harp mike to

good effect – benefited greatly from the more direct production. Even the lyrics reflected this new departure, the unknown quantities of a stranger's glance setting the band on the way to the best adventure in years.

Look out for a Bob Clearmountain remix on the CD single (8925072), while no less than four different mixes appeared on a promo-only sampler CD: 'Teddy Riley Radio Remix'/'Teddy Riley Extended Remix'/'Teddy Riley Dub Remix'/'Joe The Butcher Club Remix' (DPRO-14155). The single also included 'The Storm' (originally titled 'Idletown Prison'), one of several out-takes from the 'Voodoo Lounge' sessions, and 'So Young' (mixed by Chris Kimsey).

YOU GOT ME ROCKING

"We approached most of the songs by performing live in the studio and it worked really well," said an obviously chuffed Jagger. 'You Got Me Rocking' bears that out, capturing more than a little of the first-take excitement heard all over the band's début album.

Guest bassist Darryl Jones once worked with Miles Davis, so the driving minimalism he contributed here might have been out of character, but provided the perfect accompaniment to Watts' tub-thumping. And thanks to the production, Keith's 'mystery guitar' and Ronnie's slide rarely sounded so good together – the break was unexpectedly more evocative of Jefferson Airplane's Jorma Kaukonen, *circa* '69, than of Chuck Berry.

The second single from the album, it was backed with 'Jump On Top Of Me', an out-take from the sessions.

SPARKS WILL FLY

What better way to kick off a song about pyromania than with the sound of a lit match? Why, the band were even relaxed enough to draw on that old demonic imagery once more: the sleeve's centre spread depicted a decidedly Gothic scene called 'Satan's Play Room', and the album title itself seemed to flirt playfully with old Stones mythology.

THE WORST

One of Richards' most satisfying country-rock excursions, 'The Worst' found Frankie Gavin on fiddle, Ron Wood on pedal steel, and some uncharacteristic Jagger harmonies. Don Was secured a tremendous rhythm track from Watts and Jones, and Keith, who took two days out during the sessions to work with country legend George Jones, croaked his "I've been a bad, bad boy"-type lyric with typical conviction.

NEW FACES

This was probably the first time the word 'indolent' cropped up in a Stones lyric. 'New Faces', a title which carries with it unfortunate associations with an old amateur talent television show, immediately evoked the mid-Sixties Stones, all harpsichords, Brian Jones' recorder and Marianne Faithfull's regal folksiness.

"There's nothing wrong with playing 16th century ballads... It's a beautiful form to express yourself in," said Jagger. "Especially if you're English. It comes very naturally." That didn't explain why the Stones decided to revisit some old sounds, or how they managed to carry off such a nostalgic exercise without lapsing into self-conscious stuffiness.

MOON IS UP

The riff, the guitar sound, even the opening line ("The moon is up, the sun is down", a variant on The Beatles' 'Dear Prudence') all seemed to signify 1968. Ron Wood's pedal steel, fed through a wah-wah pedal, and Jagger's oddly-treated voice, seemed to result from a genuine desire to achieve new sounds, rather than flick the same 'effects' switch that everyone else was using.

The song, which featured backing vocalists Bobby Womack and the dependable Bernard Fowler, didn't quite equal the sum of its parts, but read against the backdrop of the last fifteen years, it sounded only marginally short of genius.

OUT OF TEARS

'Fool To Cry' and 'Angie', the band's big Seventies ballads, polarised their audiences in a way that a song like 'Ruby Tuesday' never did a decade earlier. 'Out Of Tears' was the most

remarkable track on the album, harking back to the days when songwriters could produce that tingle factor without the accompanying finger-down-the-throat.

For the first time, Chuck Leavell played with the same kind of unflappable majesty that made Nicky Hopkins so vital in bringing the best out of Jagger and Richards' work. David Campbell's string arrangement was low-key but effective, though it was the irresistible chorus and Jagger's most moving vocal performance for God-knows-how-many years which pulled the song off. While the Eighties Stones often made you question why you ever liked the band in the first place, 'Out Of Tears' proved that, in the Nineties, they were quite capable of reminding you exactly why.

I GO WILD

Even the tacky string synths of the previous decade had been ditched, as Chuck Leavell's B-3 organ gives this one-riff'll-do number with the three-word chorus more dignity than it would have been afforded several years earlier. Though recorded, like the rest of the album, at U2's Windmill Lane Studios, Dublin, this Jagger-initiated song wasn't mixed by Don Was at the A&M Studios in Hollywood, but by Bob Clearmountain in New York.

BRAND NEW CAR

There's a suspicion that the band played its best hand first, as 'Brand New Car' ushers in a string of songs that don't quite maintain the momentum on the best start to a Stones album for years. A strange Mark Isham trumpet motif helps save the track.

SWEETHEARTS TOGETHER

Marianne Faithfull's recent contention that there was a definite sexual dimension to the Jagger/Richards relationship gave a new twist to this Everlys-like ballad, which found the pair face-to-face and celebrating their "two hearts together as one".

Appropriately, perhaps, the song was set to a Latin rhythm, with Flaco Jimenez on accordion and Ronnie again on pedal steel. Love makes sweet music.

SUCK ON THE JUGULAR

There was a time when the Stones almost swamped themselves out of existence with guest musicians. 'Voodoo Lounge' was a far more intimate affair than usual, with the five-piece rehearsing at Ron Wood's house in Kildare, before taking the songs into the studio. This hard funk number was the exception, with no less than twelve musicians in tow. It probably grew out of a studio jam, with Mick doing the lion's share of the work.

BLINDED BY RAINBOWS

Recording in Ireland no doubt concentrated Jagger's mind on the terrorism which has wrecked the six counties in the north for the past twenty-five years. The 'rainbows' are the two conflicting ideals in what political scientists describe as a zero-sum – no-win – situation; the 'blinding' being the pursuit of violent means with no concern for the human tragedies such actions inevitably bring. Nostalgics should note how Jagger still sings 'rainbows' in exactly the same way as he did in 1967 on 'She's A Rainbow'.

BABY BREAK IT DOWN

This one had Keith Richards stamped all over it, so much so that Jagger even sang it through the eyes of his partner. Wood's pedal steel, which came into its own on this album, is used to good effect, though the song hinges on the chorus, where backing vocalists Ivan Neville and Bernard Fowler added considerable muscle.

THRU AND THRU

The fact that a hefty fifteen songs were deemed suitable for inclusion, and that all of them were credited to Jagger/Richards, was an obvious show of strength. But there was no doubting whose song this was, from the earnest love-struck lyric, the unflappable build-up and that unmistakable rasping vocal. This was largely Keith's show, though Charlie's cannonball-shot drum beats were an unusual treat.

MEAN DISPOSITION

'Mean Disposition' sounds more like it should have been saved for a Keith solo album title than used for this flighty rocker, complete with Stu-like touches from Leavell. It wasn't a classic finale, but Richards' Berry-ish break, and a chorus which sounded remarkably like it had been lifted from 'Aftermath', maintained the interest.

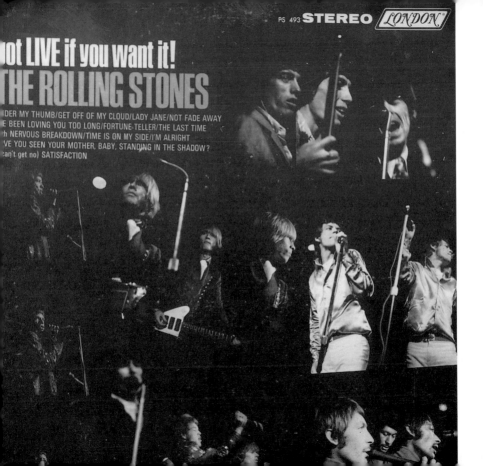

PS 493 **STEREO** *London*

ot **LIVE** if you want it!
THE ROLLING STONES

NDER MY THUMB/GET OFF OF MY CLOUD/LADY JANE/NOT FADE AWAY
E BEEN LOVING YOU TOO LONG/FORTUNE-TELLER/THE LAST TIME
h NERVOUS BREAKDOWN/TIME IS ON MY SIDE/I'M ALRIGHT
VE YOU SEEN YOUR MOTHER, BABY, STANDING IN THE SHADOW?
can't get no) SATISFACTION

Part Four
The Rolling Stones Live

There was a time when Keith Richards used to say he went to pieces whenever the band weren't touring. He'd be a broken man now if he hadn't modified his view over the years. But when the Stones do go out on tour, they don't do it in half measures, taking with them dozens of temporary employees, a fleet of trucks and some preposterous idea for a stage set. Others, of course, preferred it when they played small venues, like the Royal Albert Hall...

GOT LIVE IF YOU WANT IT!

(LONDON 820 137-2, RELEASED NOVEMBER 1966)

Intro/Under My Thumb/Get Off Of My Cloud/Lady Jane/Not Fade Away (Norman Petty/Charles Hardin)/I've Been Loving You Too Long (To Stop Now) (Otis Redding/Jerry Butler)/Fortune Teller (Naomi Neville)/The Last Time/19th Nervous Breakdown/Time Is On My Side (Jerry Ragovoy)/I'm Alright/Have You Seen Your Mother, Baby, Standing In The Shadow?/(I Can't Get No) Satisfaction.

For many years, this was the major oddity in the Stones' back catalogue. Deemed unsuitable for British release, it appeared in the States and in Europe in November 1966, only surfacing here occasionally in the import racks. With the CD reissues conforming to the US London catalogue, it's never been easier to find than now.

The publicity stated that the album was recorded at the infamous September 23, 1966, Royal Albert Hall performance, where the band were forced to halt the show for ten minutes after a stage invasion. In fact, just three songs, 'Under My Thumb', 'The Last Time' and 'Satisfaction', together with the manic stage introduction ("It's all about to happen! Let's hear it for the fan-tas-tic Rollin' Stones!"), were taken from that show.

The rest of the material derived from concerts in Newcastle-on-Tyne on October 1 ('Get

Off Of My Cloud', '19th Nervous Breakdown'), and Bristol on the 7th ('Lady Jane', 'Not Fade Away', 'Time Is On My Side', 'I'm Alright' and 'Have You Seen Your Mother, Baby').

So what are two mysterious cover versions, 'Fortune Teller' and 'I've Been Loving You Too Long', doing on the record? And why are the crowd noises only audible in one channel?

Quite simply, because both were cast-off studio recordings, masquerading (rather badly, it has to be said) as in-concert material. 'Fortune Teller' dated back as far as August 1963, when the band taped it for a potential follow-up to 'Come On'. Originally a 1962 US R&B hit for Benny Spellman, the Stones recorded it at Decca's West Hampstead Studios, and it was scheduled to back 'Poison Ivy' as their second 45 before that plan was shelved. 'Fortune Teller' (minus screams) made a surreptitious appearance on the 'Saturday Club' various artists compilation in 1964.

'I've Been Loving You Too Long' was one of several soul covers taped at the 'Satisfaction' sessions in May 1965. This tortured, deep soul ballad had been a hit for Redding earlier that year, and the general opinion was that while Otis could cover

'Satisfaction' (adding the horns Richards always maintained the song needed), for the suburban upstarts to cover one of Redding's finest... the nerve! Yet there was something equally moving about the Stones' version: probably a mixture of Jagger's nakedly exposed fragility as he attempted to 'do' Otis, and the oddly haunting effect of the dubbed screams battling it out with the instrumental backing.

Those two songs weren't the only doctoring on the record. 'Lady Jane', '19th Nervous Breakdown', 'I'm Alright' and 'Have You Seen Your Mother, Baby' all benefited from studio overdubs, although in the case of the latter, trying to recreate the song's opening chaos by manually slowing down the tape was probably one of the strangest decisions ever taken in a recording studio.

In fact, the decision to release the album at all seems, in hindsight, extraordinary. Out of time, out of tune, out of breath and badly recorded, 'Got Live If You Want It!' is a cacophonous artefact from the days when audiences were louder than the group's amplification, and the absence of monitors meant that musicians were forced to walk on stage with a small instrument and large helpings of blind faith. Many fans just wouldn't have it any other way.

Note: the American-only ABKCO CD release (74931) includes a different version of 'Under My Thumb' and a fuller introduction.

GET YER YA-YA'S OUT!

(LONDON 820 131-2, RELEASED SEPTEMBER 1970)

Jumpin' Jack Flash/Carol (Chuck Berry)/Stray Cat Blues/Love In Vain (traditional: arranged Jagger/Richards)/Midnight Rambler/Sympathy For The Devil/Live With Me/Little Queenie (Chuck Berry)/Honky Tonk Women/Street Fighting Man.

There are great live albums, and then there's 'Get Yer Ya-Ya's Out!', a near-perfect document from their 1969 US tour which started out as the biggest rock'n'roll party on earth and ended in Altamont, the free concert that brought the decade to a close with a large, decidedly black full-stop.

The album was recorded over two nights at New York's Madison Square Garden, on November 27 and 28, 1969 (excepting 'Love In Vain', taped at Baltimore on the 26th),

though it must be said that some judicious post-production work was added at Olympic and Trident the following February.

This time, the crowds listened, the PA's worked with hefty efficiency, and engineer Glyn Johns had the luxury of recording it on a 16-track mobile studio. Old songs, like Chuck Berry's 'Carol' and 'Little Queenie' were turned inside out and treated as contemporary rock, rather than archaic rock'n'roll numbers; the recent hits assaulted as much as they entertained; and two songs, 'Sympathy For The Devil' and 'Midnight Rambler' were dramatically rearranged, as if the band instinctively knew what horrors lay just around the corner. More than that, the production was as good as you'll ever hear on a live rock record, venomous and served without too many frills. Richards sounded as dangerous as he'd begun to look, while Mick Taylor belied his inexperience with the performance of a lifetime, particularly on 'Devil' and the closing 'Street Fighting Man'.

The original plan was to release 'Ya-Ya's' as a double set, with side-long contributions from support acts B.B. King and Ike and Tina Turner, but contractual difficulties put paid to that. Instead, expect forty minutes' worth of evidence that verifies the boast at the start of the album that proclaimed the Stones as the 'greatest rock'n'roll band in the world'. No doubt about that on this evidence.

LOVE YOU LIVE

(CBS CDCBS 450208-2; 2-CDS, MARCH 1977)

Intro: Excerpt From 'Fanfare For The Common Man' (Aaron Copland)/Honky Tonk Women/If You Can't Rock Me-Get Off Of My Cloud/Happy/Hot Stuff/Star Star/Tumbling Dice/Fingerprint File/You Gotta Move (Fred McDowell/Davis)/You Can't Always Get What You Want/Mannish Boy (Melvin London/Ellas McDaniel/McKinley Morganfield)/Crackin' Up (Ellas McDaniel)/Little Red Rooster (Willie Dixon)/Around And Around (Chuck Berry)/ It's Only Rock'n'Roll/Brown Sugar/Jumpin' Jack Flash/Sympathy For The Devil.

The tone for 'Love You Live' was set as early as on 'Honky Tonk Women'. Within seconds of the opening guitar riff, the audience had undermined the song by their pedestrian clapping, the production was lightweight, and while Richards played as only he can, Ronnie

Wood – visual asset though he was – was a largely ineffective foil. Most damming of all, little of the tension which made 'Ya-Ya's' so intoxicating was in evidence.

It was showbusiness as usual as Jagger straddled his inflatable penis, bounced around the specially-constructed star-shaped stage, while the rest of the band became bit players in a spectacle that was now bigger than the music. Other bit players – Billy Preston, Ian Stewart and Ollie Brown failed to fill the gaps, and versions of recent material like 'Hot Stuff' and 'Fingerprint File' were exposed as painfully inadequate for the task of maintaining the band's impeccable live reputation.

By opening the late Spring 1976 tour with an excerpt from Aaron Copland's 'Fanfare For The Common Man', the Stones sought to emphasise the import of the evening's entertainment, but the overall effect was akin to Presley's adoption of Strauss's 'Also Sprach Zarathustra' – an increasingly desperate attempt to mask a descent into caricature. These recordings, culled from the early June shows at the Pavilion De Paris, were apparently the cream of some 150 hours' worth of material.

Some face was saved on the four tracks recorded at the hastily-arranged performance at the El Mocambo, in Toronto, Canada. The choice of location was integral to the purpose, which was to recapture the sweaty intimacy of the band's club days. Held over two nights, on March 4 and 5, 1977, just days after Richards' drug bust, the shows provided a fine excuse to dust off many of the songs which the band first played during their months in the London R&B clubs. 'Mannish Boy' was a driving replication of Muddy Waters' 1955 Chess original; 'Crackin' Up' accentuated Bo Diddley's song with a reggae rhythm, while 'Around And Around' and 'Little Red Rooster' were emotional reruns of two evergreens from their first flushes of success. Two slide guitars failed to recreate the very real aura of Southern state mystique so effectively captured on their original 'Rooster', but they could hardly go wrong with Chuck Berry's 'Around And Around', with Richards bending his two-note Berry chords as if his life depended on it. He later remarked that the shows "felt just like another Sunday gig at the Crawdaddy". It was a welcome respite from the inhospitable surrounds of the large European venues, but there was more ungodly giganticism round the corner.

STILL LIFE
(AMERICAN CONCERT 1981)
(CBS CDCBS 450204-2, RELEASED JUNE 1982)

(Intro) Take The 'A' Train (performed by Duke Ellington & His Orchestra) (B. Strayhom)/Under My Thumb/Let's Spend The Night Together/Shattered/ Twenty Flight Rock (N. Fairchild)/Going To A Go-Go (William Robinson/Warren Moore/Marvin Tarplin/Robert Rogers)/Let Me Go/Time Is On My Side (Norman Meade)/Just My Imagination (Running Away With Me) (Norman Whitfield/Barrett Strong)/Start Me Up/(I Can't Get No) Satisfaction)/(outro) Star Spangled Banner (performed by Jimi Hendrix) (traditional: arranged Jimi Hendrix).

Measured in purely financial terms, the 'Still Life' world tour was a resounding success, playing from late 1981 in America, winding up in Europe by the middle of 1982. This album, drawn from two shows recorded during the American leg, at Meadowlands Arena, New Jersey, and the Sun Devil Stadium, Tempe, Arizona, was about as inspiring as seeing the band from the wrong end of Wembley Stadium with a team of six foot six rugby players blocking the view.

The emphasis was on "havin' a few beers, smokin' a few joints", as Jagger announced before launching into a lame 'Let's Spend The Night Together'. The good-time camaraderie did not translate well onto disc, and even the presence of two songs not previously tackled by the band – Smokey Robinson's 'Going To A Go-Go' (issued on single, backed by a version of 'Beast Of Burden' recorded on the same tour) and Eddie Cochran's 'Twenty Flight Rock', failed to elevate the album.

The single most interesting thing about 'Still Life' was the inclusion of Jagger/Richards material dating back to the Sixties, which hinted that the impasse with Allen Klein had been partly healed. The band never looked as out-of-sorts in bandanas, gaudy sports gear and ill-chosen jaded rock chic as they did in the accompanying *Let's Spend The Night Together* film. Thanks, but no thanks.

FLASHPOINT
(CBS 468 135-2, RELEASED APRIL 1991)

(Intro) Continental Drift/Start Me Up/Sad Sad Sad/Miss You/Rock And A Hard Place/Ruby Tuesday/You Can't Always Get

What You Want/Factory Girl/Can't Be Seen/Little Red Rooster (Willie Dixon)/Paint It Black/ Sympathy For The Devil/Brown Sugar/Jumpin' Jack Flash/Satisfaction/ Sex Drive/Highwire.

On the face of it, this document from the 'Steel Wheels'/'Urban Jungle' tour of 1989/90 was 'Still Life' Mark two, hailing from a venue big enough to fill the population of a medium-sized town, and taped (again by Bob Clearmountain, though produced by The Glimmer Twins in association with Chris Kimsey) in such a way that all the guts was left on the stage.

Two albums and two films from the band's last two tours rankled a bit, but 'Flashpoint' was marginally more forgivable. Perhaps it was the brave stabs at songs they'd rarely performed live before, like 'Ruby Tuesday', 'Factory Girl' and 'Paint It Black', which gave it the edge. Perhaps it was the humorous insertion of the "'Paint It Black', you devils!" cry from a devout audience member, lifted direct from 'Ya-Ya's'. Perhaps it was Eric Clapton's surprise appearance on slide for 'Little Red Rooster'. Or perhaps it was the feeling that the Stones had finally settled into middle age

with grace, attempting to do their greatest hits justice without overdoing the 'still life in the old dogs yet' bit.

Two new studio tracks tacked onto the end of the set were attempts to do just that. Recorded at the Hit Factory, London, in January 1991, 'Highwire' was inspired by the Gulf War, then dramatically descended into all-out conflict, while 'Sex Drive' was the 'Hot Stuff' riff, only funkier and dripping in horns.

Early pressings of the 'Flashpoint' CD came with a limited edition interview CD. Also look out for live versions of 'Play With Fire', 'Undercover', '2000 Light Years From Home' and 'I Just Want To Make Love To You'; a 'London Mix' of 'Winning Ugly VI', produced by Chris Kimsey; a full length version of 'Highwire'; and four remixes of 'Sex Drive' (Single Edit/Club Version/Dirty Hands Mix/Edited Club Version) spread across the various CD singles drawn from the album. Another song taped on the tour, 'Gimme Shelter', turned up as part of the EMI/Food 'Gimme Shelter' project to help the homeless in 1993.

The best of the Rolling Stones

Jump Back

'71 '93

Part Five

Compilations

THE DECCA YEARS

There are three notable compilations covering the Decca era. By far the most essential is the 'The Singles Collection: The London Years', already discussed in the context of the singles. This contains every UK and US A- and B-side, including (due to the fact that they were originally recorded while still under contract to Decca) 'Brown Sugar' and 'Wild Horses'. Some post-1971 45s are also included, most notably material from 'Metamorphosis'.

Two other compilations, 'Hot Rocks 1964-1971' (ABKCO 820 140-2) and 'More Hot Rocks (Big Hits & Fazed Cookies)' (ABKCO 820 143-2), have been reactivated on CD, and marketed for UK consumption. The latter, at least, contains one or two unexpected surprises, including revealing stereo takes of 'Dandelion', 'We Love You', and 'I Can't Be Satisfied'.

'Metamorphosis', the only collection of previously unreleased material from the archive, is still unavailable on CD. A fair por-

tion of the songs were Andrew Oldham-instigated demos for others, but there is some interesting work from the late Sixties, including a version of Stevie Wonder's 'I Don't Know Why'.

ATLANTIC AND AFTER

The most obvious point-of-entry for the best of the Stones' post-1971 work is 'Jump Back: The Best Of The Rolling Stones '71-93' (Virgin CDV 2726), issued in November 1993. The fact that it isn't chronological is less problematic in the age of the programmable CD, while the inability to include every song issued on single in the UK between those years is probably a blessing.

Still around are three titles issued on CD during the CBS era. 'Made In The Shade' (CBS 450201 2) takes the story up to 1974, a ten-track collection that could probably do with being expanded by Virgin to lend it more authority.

'Sucking In The Seventies' (CBS CDCBS 450205 2) picked up from where 'Shade' left off, its ten selections covering the period between 'Black And Blue' and 'Emotional Rescue'. In amongst the hits were three oddities: 'Everything Is Turning To Gold' originally backed the US 'Shattered' single; while the live version of 'When The Whip Comes Down' and 'If I Was A Dancer (Dance Pt. 2)' were both exclusive to the set.

Finally, 'Rewind (1971-84)' (CBS CDCBS 4501992 2) takes the story up to 1984 with 13 tracks from 'Sticky Fingers' right through to 'Undercover', but offers no alternative items.

Index

5/02 (44191)